CORETTA SCOTT KING

Keeper of the Dream

Sondra Henry & Emily Taitz

—**Contemporary Women Series**—

ENSLOW PUBLISHERS, INC.

Bloy St. and Ramsey Ave.   P.O. Box 38
Box 777   Aldershot
Hillside, N.J. 07205   Hants GU12 6BP
U.S.A.   U.K.

jB / KING / (Coretta Scott) / H

Acknowledgements

We would like to thank the following people for their help in researching the life of Coretta Scott King: Hilary Marcus, research and photo research assistant; Idella Childs; Professor David Epstein; Tamar Taitz Fields; Robert Fields; Gail Garfinkel; Dr. Edward I. Henry; Beni Ivey; Steve Klein; Sally Plotkin Lifschitz; Ruth Dembo Odell; Marcia Shapiro; Flip Schulke; Ari Taitz; Mimi Taitz; and Harry Wachtel.

Also our thanks to the archivists and librarians of Antioch College Alumni Archives, Marion-Perry County Library, Martin Luther King, Jr. Center for Nonviolent Social Change, New England Conservatory of Music, and Arthur and Elizabeth Schlesinger Library at Radcliffe College.

Library of Congress Cataloging-in-Publication Data

Henry, Sondra.
    Coretta Scott King: keeper of the dream / Sondra Henry & Emily Taitz.
        p. cm. — (Contemporary women series)
    Includes bibliographical references and index.
    Summary: Traces the life and accomplishments of the civil rights leader and widow of Dr. Martin Luther King.
    ISBN 0-89490-334-9
    1. King, Coretta Scott, 1927 –   —Juvenile literature. 2. King, Martin Luther, Jr., 1929–1968—Juvenile literature. 3. Afro–Americans—Biography—Juvenile literature. 4. Civil rights workers—United States—Biography—Juvenile literature. [1. King, Coretta Scott, 1927– . 2. King, Martin Luther, Jr., 1929–1968. 3. Civil rights workers. 4. Afro-Americans—Biography.] I. Taitz, Emily. II. Title. III. Series.
    E185.97.K47H46   1992
    323'.092—dc20   91-31082
    [B]

Printed in the United States of America

10 9 8 7 6 5 4 3 2

Illustration Credits:
Antiochiana Collection, Antioch College, p. 21; Bethune-Cookman College Archives, p. 91; The Bettmann Archive, p. 39; © Bettye Lane, pp. 4, 94; Dexter Ave. King Memorial Baptist Church, p. 32; © Diana Mara Henry, 1978, p. 104; Donna Binder, Impact Visuals, p. 108; Edward I. Henry, M.D., p. 105; © Flip Shulke, pp. 53, 66, 68, 77; ©1989 John Jernegan, Impact Visuals, p. 9; New England Conservatory Archives, pp. 24, 28, 41, 47, 97; © 1988 Rick Reinhard, Impact Visuals, p. 112; Sally Plotkin Lifschitz, pp. 17, 18, 19; Smithsonian Institution, Washington, D.C., p. 34; Standard Oil (N.J.) Collection, University of Louisville Photographic Archives, p. 12; United Nations, p. 106; United Nations/ Y. Nagata, p. 102.

Cover Illustration: Globe Photos, Inc.

Contents

Coretta Scott King

Introduction
"The Blessing of His Life"

Coretta Scott King stood proudly in the Rose Garden of the White House. She was surrounded by Vice-President George Bush, Senator Edward Kennedy and Jesse Jackson, prominent members of the United States government or of the black community. Also present were her children and members of her family.

With great emotion, Coretta watched as President Ronald Reagan picked up a pen and signed his name. His signature established a national holiday in honor of her late husband, Dr. Martin Luther King, Jr.

Dr. King was the only person in the history of the United States—besides George Washington—to be honored with a national, legal holiday. The achievement represented years of hard work by his widow. Joined by countless other African Americans, Coretta Scott King had devoted herself to achieving national recognition for her husband. Now, as she rose to speak, there was a respectful silence.

"Thank God for the blessing of his life and his leadership and his commitment," said Coretta. "May we make ourselves worthy to carry on his dream and create the love community."

Coretta had kept her husband's dreams alive. She had continued the fight for equality, expanding it to include her own ideas of peace and justice.

"All right-thinking people, all right-thinking Americans," she asserted, "are joined in spirit with us this day . . . "

For Coretta Scott King, the signing was a milestone on a long and continuing journey toward a just society. Throughout her life, Coretta has clung to the same goals: "to be treated as an equal" and "to do something for humanity." While working toward those goals, she has helped change our nation.

Coretta's story began in a small wooden farmhouse in rural Alabama, where she was born. Her difficult and challenging youth helped shape the woman she would become. Her experiences prepared her for a life of struggle and accomplishment.

1

"As Good As Anyone Else"

Father worked hard to make enough money so they could have a bigger home, right here in Perry County, Alabama. Then Coretta, or Corrie as her family called her, and her older sister Edythe would have their own room. They would not have to share the one bedroom with their parents and younger brother.

The new house would have a vegetable garden, too. The girls could help Mother plant in the spring. Late in summer and through the fall, they could pick the squash, turnips, dandelion greens, tomatoes, and corn and cook them up for dinner.

Coretta was a slim, lively girl. She had dark eyes, thick, black hair that she wore down to her shoulders, and honey-colored skin. Her high cheekbones hinted at the Native American heritage passed down from her mother's father. Corrie's family remembered that even as a child she was a fighter. "Mother said I was the meanest girl," said Coretta. "I used to fight all the time."

When Coretta was ten, the family finally did move. They left the tiny two-room house that her father had built and settled into a big six-room farmhouse. For the first time, they had a living room with new furniture. Coretta and Edythe had their own bedroom.

Coretta's father, Obadiah Scott, had labored for that house. It was not easy to get ahead, especially when you were a black man living in Alabama in the 1920s. It was even more difficult when you started out with no money and little education.

From the time Obie Scott and his wife, Bernice, were married, they had struggled to achieve a better life. When Coretta, the Scott's second child, was born on April 27, 1927, the United States was enjoying a surge of economic prosperity. In 1929, however, the stock market crashed. Businesses were failing, and people everywhere were out of jobs.

During the Great Depression, as the 1930s were called, even middle-class white people were going hungry. For black people, making a living was always harder. But Obie somehow managed to keep going. The Scotts were determined that their two daughters, Edythe and Coretta, and their son, Obie Leonard, would be educated.

Father worked during the day in a sawmill. He also learned to be a barber, and he cut people's hair in the evenings. When he had saved enough money to buy a truck, Obie used it to haul logs and timber for the white mill owner.

Bernice was busy, too. She tended their farm and the animals and took care of their children. The Scotts saved every penny, depriving themselves of any luxury.

Although their financial situation was improving, Coretta's family still had to work hard. Father owed money to a local white businessman who had helped him make the payments on his truck. Obie Scott never missed a payment. He even paid one hundred dollars extra when the white man insisted that the debt was not yet paid.

Coretta remembered the very day in 1939 when the final payment was made. Her father took them all into the nearby town of Marion to celebrate and buy whatever they wanted.

Growing up as a black child in the South was never easy.

Although Coretta's mother always told her that she was "just as good as anyone else," life often taught another lesson. By the time Corrie was ready to begin school, she already understood that she was different than the white children.

In her autobiography, Coretta told about not being able to buy a soda at the lunch counter in Marion or even stand in the same line as the white children for an ice cream cone. There was a door, all the way in the back by the kitchen, where the black children had to go and wait. Even if Corrie was first in line, she had to wait until every white child out front got their ice cream before she could get hers.

At those times Coretta's mother would patiently explain that white people were ignorant and didn't understand. Blacks would

Some southern black women like Bernice Scott worked their own farmland.

9

just have to prove they could achieve as much as whites, that they could be as good or better than whites in spite of the unfair laws.

"You get an education and try to be somebody," her mother told Coretta. "Then you won't have to be kicked around by anybody, and you won't have to depend on anyone for your livelihood—not even on a man."

Many black girls heard these words from their mothers. It was in strong contrast to the "romance, marriage, motherhood" bombardment that young white women heard in those years.

Coretta listened to her mother's advice and worked hard. Her brother Obie Leonard recalled that his sister "always tried to excel in everything she did. And she made good marks," he added.

However, even going to school in the morning made it hard to remember that she was as good as any white child. Coretta and her sister and brother had to walk three miles to the all-black school at Heiberger, a crossroads village. The white children were bused right into Marion. Their modern school had classrooms with blackboards, and bathrooms right in the building. Coretta's school had only one big room where everyone, from first to sixth grade, was taught together. There were only two teachers.

In spite of these difficult conditions, Coretta graduated at the top of her class. When the time came for her to enter seventh grade, Bernice arranged for both Corrie and Edythe to go to a black school ten miles away in Marion.

Marion was much too far to walk back and forth every day. And again, there was no bus for the black students. Coretta and Edythe had to pay to board with a black family.

Obie and Bernice had only a few years of schooling themselves but insisted "The most important thing now is to get an education."

Somehow, the Scotts managed to scrape together the money for school. One of the ways Corrie and her sister helped meet the expenses was to work picking cotton. The first time Coretta worked as a cotton picker she was only ten years old.

Every year, when the cotton crop came in, black workers lined up outside the big farms to be hired as pickers. Once hired, each adult or child was assigned to a row and given a big burlap sack to store the picked cotton. The sack, worn over the shoulder, was weighed by the foreman at the end of the work day.

At first, the work did not seem so difficult, and the long burlap sack was light. But as it slowly filled with the white, fluffy balls of cotton, the bags got heavier. Still, you were paid according to how much cotton you picked, so a worker could not slow down too much.

Coretta remembered, "I was always very strong, and I made a very good cotton picker."

Even the few cents a bag that Corrie earned helped the family. After many days of picking cotton, there might be enough money to pay for a bolt of bright-colored fabric. She would bring it to her grandmother, Mollie McMurry, to be made into a new dress for her to wear for school or church. Grandmother McMurry sewed all the clothes for Coretta and her sister.

The school in Marion was named the Lincoln School. It was a black school that had been founded by the American Missionary Association just after the Civil War. At that time white teachers were sent from the North to teach the children of former slaves. In the 1940s it was still a black semi-private school with high standards and modern facilities. There were real desks instead of the wooden benches Corrie was used to at the Heiberger school. Each classroom had a blackboard, and there were different teachers for each subject.

Black families from all over the South who valued education sent their children to the Lincoln School. They paid only a small sum of money. Here, for the first time, Corrie was taught by white as well as black teachers. Some of the teachers were from the northern part of the United States. They told Coretta and the other students that African Americans in northern cities did not have to

Like the woman in this photo, Coretta and her sister picked cotton. They worked to raise extra money for their family.

move to the back of the bus or use different public bathrooms. They could eat in the same restaurants as white people did; they could go to the movies and sit wherever they wanted.

In Alabama Corrie always paid her bus fare and then walked to the back door of the bus and found a seat at the back. There were waiting areas and water fountains in the bus station marked "colored" and "white." It was against the law for a black person to drink from the "whites only" fountain.

These segregation laws were accepted ideas in the South up until the 1960s. Americans had a special name for laws of segregation: Jim Crow. The name originated from a song and dance routine about an African American named Jim Crow.

The idea of being free from segregation laws appealed to Coretta. But for now, Corrie had much to learn at the Lincoln School, where she had many friends.

The family she stayed with was kind to her. For a short time, Coretta earned some of her rent money by doing housework for a white woman. Evenings were spent on homework. Even though she missed her family, her activities kept her from being too homesick.

It was at this school that Coretta learned to play the piano. A wonderful music teacher, Olive J. Williams, recognized Coretta's musical talent. Ms. Williams was a fine musician and a graduate of Howard University, one of the best black universities in the United States. She gave Coretta piano lessons and her first formal voice instruction.

Coretta had always loved music. She sang in her church choir from the time she was a little girl. On their phonograph, her parents often played records of the great black jazz singers as well as popular songs and gospel music. But they never could hope for a piano of their own because it was too costly.

Studying the piano was one of the most exciting things that Coretta did at the Lincoln School. She also sang in the chorus and learned to play the trumpet.

Coretta's sister Edythe also sang. She was a member of a special singing group at Lincoln called the Lincoln School Little Chorus. In 1941, this group performed at some midwestern colleges, including Antioch College at Yellow Springs, Ohio. The singing tour helped open a door of opportunity for both Edythe and Coretta.

When Antioch College decided to accept blacks for the first time, they sent a letter to the Lincoln School inviting students to apply. Edythe sent in her application and was accepted.

The year 1942 had been a good year for Coretta. She played the piano and rehearsed the choir at the Mount Tabor Church. Not only did she enjoy singing, but she also wrote musical programs for school and church. She dreamed of a career in music, modeling herself after her beloved music teacher Olive J. Williams.

The year was almost over when Corrie received a telephone call from a family friend. Something terrible had happened. Her home in Heiberger had burned down, Coretta was told.

Coretta's parents and brother had escaped the fire. They were staying at Grandfather McMurry's farm.

There was nothing left, Coretta learned. Their family home, the result of so much working and saving, was now gone. Some charred wood and their old tin cooking pots, blackened from the smoke, were all that remained. Clothing, furniture, the precious records that Coretta remembered hearing from the time she was a baby—everything had been burned.

By 1942, Coretta's father had begun to do well. He was the only black man who owned three trucks in his community. He was planning to start his own business. Obie had not paid any attention when white men harassed him and reported him for reckless driving. Even when they threatened to kill him, Obie stood his ground.

Coretta always worried about her father's safety. She knew there were many people throughout the South who didn't think black people should be allowed to succeed. Perhaps a white man had objected to the Scott family's "uppity" ways and decided to teach them a lesson by setting fire to their house.

The Scotts would never know whether the fire was deliberately set or not. Although they believed that it was not an accident, they could not prove it. Sympathetic white people advised Obie to ask for an investigation, but he knew it would do no good.

Corrie was fifteen years old at the time of the fire. She too understood that white people controlled Perry County and the nearby town of Marion. Coretta later wrote: " . . . really no one cared about what happened to black people."

She also knew that many whites did not feel comfortable about blacks becoming educated. They did not believe it was natural for "coloreds," as they were called then, to be anything but servants or workers. When Coretta's father was a laborer, when he worked as a barber cutting black men's hair, and when at night he hauled logs for white owners, they didn't mind so much. But many whites resented a black man owning his own trucks and becoming success- ful. Blacks should be kept "in their place," some whites insisted.

Coretta's mother, Bernice McMurry Scott, and the entire Mc- Murry and Scott families were prominent members of Perry County's black community. They owned their own land and were active in the Mount Tabor A.M.E. (African Methodist Episcopal) Zion Church. Coretta and her sister Edythe were both in high school and planning on college. Perhaps they should be satisfied to stay in their own world.

But the Scotts wanted more. Each one of them, in his or her own way, challenged the old, southern traditions of inequality. Ultimately, the Scotts and others like them would change some of the unfair laws of their country, but that was far in the future.

Now, after the news that her house had burned down, Coretta wondered what would happen tomorrow. Had the fire also de- stroyed her own dreams for the future?

2

"Wherever Martin Lives, I Will Live There Too"

It would take more than a fire to beat Obadiah Scott. Even a second fire, which destroyed his sawmill, would not keep him from sending his daughters off to college in the North if that was what they wanted. The house was rebuilt, and Obie continued working.

The following year, 1943, Edythe began Antioch College. The school even gave her a full scholarship, and Edythe became the first African-American student there. It seemed the most wonderful opportunity in the world. Could Corrie ever hope for the same chance?

Coretta only received a partial scholarship from the Race Relations Committee of Antioch College, but she couldn't wait to go. Her parents would manage to pay the additional two hundred dollars in fees plus her transportation to Yellow Springs.

When Coretta first arrived at the college in September 1945, she was shy and often depended on Edythe—called "Scottie" by her friends—to speak for her. In spite of her sister's glowing reports, life at a northern college was far from easy. There were only three black students in Coretta's class and only six in the entire school.

Her first year, Corrie lived in a dorm on campus. Then for a while she boarded with a black family in town to save some money. Coretta's close friend Sally Plotkin, a student from the North, remembered that Corrie had a bicycle. She rode her bike back and forth between Yellow Springs and the campus on the edge of town.

Although all the white students were friendly, Corrie never had a date during her first two years. She refused, on principle, to date the only black young man in her class. Often she found herself explaining the realities of segregation and prejudice to her white friends. They tried to understand but still tended to associate her in their minds with other blacks on campus. Corrie would gently point out how that was also a form of prejudice.

Antioch College in Yellow Springs, Ohio as it looked when Coretta first arrived. Both Coretta and her sister Edythe would attend this newly integrated college.

"She never really complained," Sally Plotkin later recalled about her friend Corrie. "She just educated us in a very nice way." Coretta had come North to avoid segregation and would not submit to what she called "social segregation." In her third year at Antioch, Coretta dated a Jewish music student for about a year. They remained friends after he graduated.

At the Lincoln School, Coretta had been an "A" student and class valedictorian. Here at Antioch, however, she found that she had an inadequate educational background. Coretta was behind most of the white students and had to work much harder to keep up.

Despite all the extra hours spent studying, Coretta found time to be active in the Antioch chapter of the NAACP (National

While at Antioch College, Coretta made many friends. Here, she is pictured with fellow student Ruth Dembo.

Coretta takes a break from studying.

Association for the Advancement of Colored People). This civil rights organization was one of the few that existed in the United States at the time. She also joined the Quaker peace groups at the college.

Antioch College offered a slightly different program than most other institutions of higher learning. Students alternated work with study, and the program usually took five years to complete. During Coretta's college years, she held several different jobs. She worked as a waitress, as a music counselor at a summer camp, in a settlement house in Cleveland, Ohio, and as a library assistant. One semester she set up a bookkeeping system for her father's new general store and earned college credit for it.

All these jobs were interesting work experiences for Coretta, but her primary focus was music and education. Corrie was the first black to major in education at Antioch College. As part of the training for music teachers, students had to do practice teaching in the Antioch model school for a year and in a Yellow Springs public school for an additional year.

Teaching at the Antioch College model school was no problem. However, when it came time to spend a year in the public school system, Coretta's application was turned down. All the teachers at the Yellow Springs schools were white.

Coretta appealed to the Antioch administration. She wanted them to intervene and insist on her having the same opportunity as the white students. The new president of the college refused.

Coretta was hurt and disappointed by this experience with overt racism. On the surface, Antioch had a policy of racial equality. Underneath, there were signs of bigotry. It was rumored that the president of the college had a black dog named "Nigger," a degrading term used for black people.

Many students and faculty encouraged Coretta to fight the Yellow Springs school board decision. Sally Plotkin also remembered the incident. Although she and some others were indignant, they knew that nothing could be done to change the decision.

Coretta as a student at Antioch College.

The college would not fight the Yellow Springs school board. They gave Coretta two alternatives. She could teach an additional year at the Antioch model school or do her practice teaching in an all-black school in Xenia, a neighboring town.

"I will not go to Xenia," she insisted, "because I came here from Alabama to be free of segregation."

Coretta taught at the Antioch school a second year. Although she was upset, she was determined not to become embittered. Years later, speaking to a new group of Antioch graduates, Coretta recalled that incident. "It did not cause me to lose faith in Antioch and its efforts to integrate blacks into the educational mainstream."

With continued encouragement from her teachers, Coretta learned violin and sang in the college chorus. Dr. Walter Anderson, the only black professor at Antioch, arranged a concert for her at a church in Springfield, Ohio, in 1948. When Coretta prepared to leave Antioch in 1951, she had gained confidence and had a new goal—to become a concert performer.

Jessie Treichler, another faculty member, had also recognized Coretta's talents. She advised her to continue her musical education at a conservatory and to apply for tuition grants.

Once Coretta was accepted at the New England Conservatory of Music in Boston, she was determined to go with or without a scholarship. She left Alabama with only her train fare and barely enough money for her expenses. On her way to Boston, she called home and learned a letter had arrived from a foundation, granting her $650 towards her tuition.

Coretta still had to work at several different jobs to earn enough for food and rent and to pay for voice lessons. She had so little money that even the twenty-five cent bus fare was too much for her. Coretta did housework for her landlady in exchange for her room and breakfast. She economized by eating fruit and crackers the rest of the day.

Despite financial difficulties, Coretta remembers her days in

Boston as one of the happiest times of her life. Social life was better in Boston, too. Black students from all the local colleges gathered informally in a few southern-style restaurants which catered to black patrons or at people's homes. Although Coretta was part of this group, she was not looking for a boyfriend. She was committed to pursuing a career as a concert singer.

But Mary Powell, a married friend, gave Coretta's telephone number to a graduate student at Boston University who wanted to meet her. His name was Martin Luther King, Jr.

The phone call was a pleasant surprise. She and Martin talked for a long time and arranged to meet, but Coretta was still doubtful. Martin was studying theology and philosophy and was a Baptist minister. Corrie was certainly not interested in being a minister's wife. That was not the kind of life she had planned for herself. Still, it couldn't hurt to see him this once.

They met for lunch, with just one hour between Coretta's classes at the conservatory. When M. L., as he was known, came to pick her up in his old car, Coretta thought that he was short and not impressive. As they talked, however, she forgot about his height and "completely revised my first impression."

The hour went by quickly. Coretta had to return to class and M. L. King drove her back. When her new acquaintance suddenly said to her, "You have everything I have ever wanted in a wife . . . character, intelligence, personality, and beauty," Coretta was a bit flustered. In spite of M. L.'s declaration of intentions, she was not at all ready to change her life for him. Yet Martin, the name by which he would later be known, interested her.

His courtship of Coretta continued from that time. They saw each other regularly and had long talks. Martin told her about his ideas on philosophy and nonviolence.

Dr. Chester Williams, a teacher at the conservatory, often saw Martin "hanging around the back of Jordan Hall, waiting for Coretta to finish a rehearsal." Corrie began to go with Martin to the

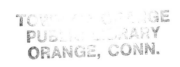

Coretta remembers her years at the New England Conservatory as one of the happiest times of her life.

Baptist church in Roxbury where he was occasionally a guest preacher. Sometimes, she was asked to sing for the congregation.

Coretta tried to resist making a commitment because she did not want to give up her career in music. The idea of being the wife of a Baptist minister was not appealing to her, either. She discussed some of these conflicting feelings with her sister Edythe.

After meeting Martin, Edythe urged Coretta to marry. But even without Edythe's advice, Coretta realized that she could not give Martin up.

David Epstein, Corrie's friend from Antioch who was also studying at the conservatory, first met Martin at a party. He remembered feeling happy for Coretta and thinking "Wow! What a guy!" David, who admired Coretta, was impressed even then with Martin's dynamic personality.

Martin believed that women were as capable as men and should hold positions of authority and influence. He wanted a wife who was intelligent and with whom he could communicate. However, he also wanted his wife to be a homemaker and mother. Coretta knew that as a concert performer this would be especially difficult.

It took Coretta several months to make the decision to marry Martin Luther King, Jr. Then they had to convince Martin's parents.

A visit to Atlanta during summer vacation introduced her to Mr. and Mrs. King, Sr., as well as to Martin's brother A.D. and A.D.'s family. The Kings lived in a large, comfortable house on Auburn Avenue. Daddy King, as he was called by almost everyone, presided over Ebenezer Baptist Church, a congregation of several thousand people. Segregation laws affected them, too, of course, but they were part of a prosperous African-American community.

In contrast, Coretta's family lived in a rural farming area in Alabama where people struggled to earn enough for food and shelter. Education was stressed and valued as a way to earn respect and escape from poverty. But in Perry County, a college education was not as common as it was among the middle-class blacks of Atlanta.

Coretta was concerned that the Kings would not accept her and knew they did not take her seriously as a prospective wife. She heard about the many girls with whom Martin had been involved and later admitted that she was a little annoyed by those stories. Coretta would have to face such gossip and rumors all her life, although she certainly did not know it at that time.

It was not until the Kings' visited Boston again that Coretta felt she was finally accepted by Martin's family. The couple began to plan for marriage, and their engagement was announced in the African-American newspaper, the *Atlanta Daily*.

The next semester, Coretta changed her major at the conservatory to music education and voice. This way she could teach music wherever she and Martin were living, and she would not have to travel in order to work.

When she decided to marry Martin, Coretta made two commitments. The first was to Martin himself. The second was that " . . . wherever Martin lives, I will live there too. Whatever he does, I will be involved."

In June 1953, Martin and Corrie were married on the lawn of the Scott home outside Marion, Alabama. Coretta wore a pale blue lace dress with matching gloves and shoes and a wreath of fresh flowers over her veil. The wedding arch was decorated with flowers picked from the Scott garden.

The ceremony was presided over by Daddy King with only one change. In the traditional church wedding, the bride promised to "love, honor, and obey" her husband. At the request of both the bride and groom, the word "obey" had been left out. Coretta and Martin would be equal partners.

After the wedding, the young couple drove off to spend their first night together. Because of the segregation laws in the South, they were not permitted to check into a hotel. Even though they had enough money, they could not walk into the lobby of a "white" hotel in Alabama. Martin and Corrie spent their wedding night at a friend's home in Marion. The next day they drove back to Atlanta and had another reception for Martin's friends.

They had no real honeymoon. Martin worked with his father as assistant pastor at Ebenezer Baptist Church, and Coretta got a summer job. In September they returned to Boston to finish school and rented their first apartment together.

Coretta had a busy schedule that final year, taking thirteen credits in one semester to finish up her degree. The many requirements included voice, piano, orchestral arrangement, and directing. Coretta also had to learn how to play other instruments, including percussion, strings, woodwinds, and brass.

In her last semester, Coretta King did student teaching in the Boston public schools. She was the only black teacher in her school, but no problem arose as it had in Ohio. "The children loved her and were most appreciative of her ability," wrote one of her supervisors. "Her manner is charming and gracious. She will make a fine teacher."

Martin was busy doing research for his doctoral thesis, attending classes, and occasionally preaching at the local Baptist churches. Still, he had more free time than Coretta and helped with the housework, laundry, and cooking. In spite of his willingness to do what was then considered women's work, Coretta understood when her young husband asserted: "I want my wife to respect me as the head of the family. I *am* the head of the family."

Coretta looked up to Martin and was proud of his self-assurance. She understood that being the chief provider was often difficult for black men because of their lack of economic opportunity.

Very quickly, that last happy year in Boston ended. Coretta's mother and Martin were there in the auditorium of the New England

Coretta smiled for this photo in 1954. The young bride received her bachelor's degeee in music education and voice that spring.

Conservatory as she received her bachelor's degree in music education.

Coretta had worked hard, but she was leaving behind a life with few dilemmas. Now she and Martin would have to make some difficult decisions: where to work and where to live.

Should they stay up North? In the North there was certainly prejudice against African Americans, but there was less obvious segregation and more opportunity for advancement. She knew that someday she would return to the South, but she was not ready to go yet.

Martin thought they should go now. The South was where their roots and their families were. They might suffer from Jim Crow laws and lack of respect from hostile whites, but they would have a chance to do the most good for their people. The South pulled Martin back. "That is where I am needed," he said.

The couple debated their decision for many days. They thought, they talked, and they prayed. Finally they agreed.

3

"Much Bigger Than Montgomery"

It was one of many decisions that Corrie would make for Martin's sake. In spite of Coretta's doubts, they would go back to the South.

People who did not live with segregation could never really understand just what it meant. At Antioch College, Coretta had to explain it to Sally and her other white friends. If they traveled South together, she could drive with them. People would assume she was their maid, Corrie told them. Once they arrived, her white friends would not be able to stay at her home. "That would mean trouble."

As Martin finished his work in Boston, he began to get invitations from black Baptist churches throughout the country. Prospective pastors were invited to give a sermon and meet the congregation. If the church members liked the pastor, an offer would be made.

Martin had several job offers, including one from his father. Daddy King wanted Martin to return to Atlanta as assistant pastor at Ebenezer Baptist Church. Then an offer came from the Dexter Avenue Baptist Church in Montgomery, Alabama, and Martin believed it was just right.

The Dexter Avenue Baptist Church was a dignified brick building with a double flight of stairs leading up to the entrance. It stood in the square opposite the state supreme court and Alabama's state capitol.

Coretta learned that the church had been built right after the Civil War, during the Reconstruction period. This was when the former African slaves first experienced freedom under white northern rule. For a brief time, with the help of the federal government, some black people bought property in downtown Montgomery. Although most of those blacks "were eventually pushed out," Coretta explained, the Dexter Avenue church remained.

The pastor's home was a seven-room wood frame house with a big front porch, comfortably furnished but somewhat run-down. The congregation promised to redecorate it before September.

Martin had told Corrie that this church met all his requirements for a job. Now that she saw it for herself, she felt more positive. "If this is what you want, I'll make myself happy in Montgomery," she promised Martin.

Coretta had no experience at being a minister's wife, but she was sensitive, intelligent, and ready to learn. By September she and Martin had settled into their Montgomery home, and Coretta was already conscious of a sense of destiny. "Even in 1954," she wrote, "I felt that my husband was being prepared—and I too—for a special role."

There are many ways to play a "special role," as Coretta learned. Later, she would urge her husband to let her share more in his activities. But in those first years, her life was home-centered. She sang in the church choir and appeared in a few local concerts. She helped Martin with secretarial work and kept house. Within a year, Coretta became pregnant with their first child.

Martin's life centered on the church. He preached a weekly sermon, attended to the needs of his congregation, and set up new committees to expand church interests.

31

The Dexter Avenue Baptist Church in Montgomery, Alabama. Martin was invited to be the pastor here in 1954.

The Dexter Avenue church was known as a "rich folks" church. Most of its members were middle-class, well-educated blacks who worked at the Alabama State College, a local college for African Americans. One of Martin's goals was to bring poorer people into his church. Everything in the South, including the churches, was completely segregated, so there were no white members.

Martin also became involved in the larger community. He joined the NAACP and the Alabama Council for Human Rights, the only interracial group in the city. Martin made a favorable impression and was soon invited to serve on the local NAACP executive committee.

Just a little more than a year after the Kings had come to Montgomery, on November 17, 1955, their first child, Yolanda Denise ("Yoki"), was born. Coretta and Martin were delighted with their new daughter, but Coretta soon found that she had to give up some outside activities to take care of her home and baby.

Although Coretta had wanted a career, she accepted Martin's wish and became a homemaker. Martin had made it clear to her that he was "the man of the family." He wanted her to remain at home and raise his children.

The Kings made friends very quickly with members of their congregation. Shortly after Martin took the post at Dexter Avenue, they met Ralph and Juanita Abernathy. Rev. Ralph Abernathy was pastor at another important church in the city. Corrie and Juanita had both grown up in Perry County, Alabama, and were about the same age. Both women had graduated from college, a major accomplishment for blacks in the South at that time.

"Because of Jim Crow we could only have dinner at home," Abernathy explained in his autobiography. "So the four of us had dinner every night, with Coretta preparing the meal one evening, Juanita the next. Conversations among the four of us would last way beyond midnight." They talked about segregation and what African Americans were doing to try to change the laws.

Outside the Kings' home on South Jackson Street, however, new events were destined to turn that talk into action. Every person, whether black or white, would be affected by these developments.

The incident that began the revolution in the South happened on a local bus as it followed its regular route through the city of Montgomery. It was December 1, 1955.

Like all the buses in Montgomery, this one divided the space for black and white passengers. The front seats were reserved for whites. Blacks were expected to sit in the back. If the bus was crowded and there were more white passengers, blacks were supposed to stand up and give their seats to white people.

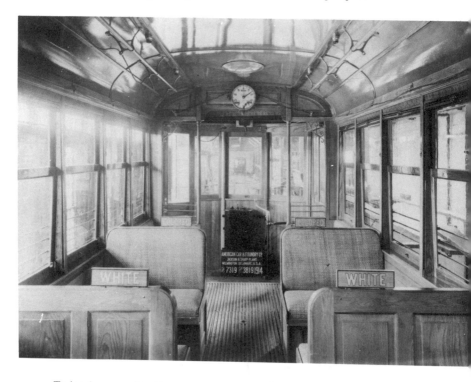

Trains, buses, and trolley cars were segregated. African Americans could sit only in the sections marked 'colored.'

Blacks resented this arrangement and tried many times to change it. Sometimes they would not get up until the driver made them leave. If blacks had cars they would not ride the buses at all.

One of the passengers on the bus that December day was an African American named Rosa Parks. She worked as a seamstress in a local department store, but was also a woman actively committed to the cause of civil rights. Mrs. Parks was on her way home from work. As more people got on, the bus became crowded. Rosa was seated in the row closest to the "whites only" section. When a few additional white passengers climbed aboard, the driver turned to her and the other blacks seated in her section. He demanded that they get up.

No one wanted to give up his seat after a long day of work. With repeated demands, the others finally did. Only Rosa Parks, who was particularly tired that night, refused. She had refused before, and she would refuse again. "My resistance to being mistreated on the buses and anywhere else was just a regular thing with me and not just that day," Parks later explained.

The white bus driver was insistent that Rosa give up her seat to the white man. Rather than allow her to remain, he stopped the bus and went out on the street to find a policeman. Rosa Parks was arrested and brought to the police station. A report was filed, and she was allowed out on bail. Trial was set for December 5.

It seemed almost as if the African-American community in Montgomery had been waiting for something like this to happen. They were anxious to test the laws of bus segregation in court. The Women's Political Council (WPC), under the leadership of Jo Ann Gibson Robinson, had already planned a boycott of the city buses because of previous incidents like this one.

The Women's Political Council was an organization of professional black women. Their goal was to register black people to vote and to improve the situation for all African Americans. When they heard of Rosa's arrest, they mobilized for action. Rosa Parks was the secretary of the local NAACP and a founder of the NAACP youth council in Montgomery. She appeared to be the perfect test case.

At first, it appeared that E. D. Nixon, head of the Progressive Democratic Association, would be the most obvious person to lead the boycott. He was well known in town for his militant stand against Jim Crow. But Nixon recognized that a minister should be the leader of the boycott. "Ministers will follow one another and then we wouldn't have to be fighting the churches to get something done," he explained.

Mr. Nixon was expressing a very important fact about black southerners. A vast majority were members of Christian churches. Because of that, the best way to organize the African-American community was to get their ministers involved.

There were other reasons why Dr. King was asked to head this new group, named the Montgomery Improvement Association (MIA). In the short time that Martin was living in Montgomery, news of his skill as an orator had spread. Many believed that speaking skills were crucial in rallying people to this cause. Also, Martin was new in town and had no enemies.

The MIA was responsible for leading what was at first to be a one-day boycott of all of Montgomery's buses. That meant informing the black community, helping people get to work without using public transportation, and negotiating with city and bus company officials. In addition, the community had to be convinced that the cause was important enough for them to make sacrifices.

Sunday night, the evening before the boycott was set to begin, Coretta and Martin sat in their living room. They talked about the events of the past few days: Martin's acceptance of the leadership role in the MIA, the modest demands of the black community, and the refusal of the city council to accept them.

Black people in Montgomery were not asking for equal rights or mixed seating on the buses. They only asked for three things.

They requested that black passengers be seated from the back toward the front on a first-come first-served basis with no seats reserved for whites. They also wanted the bus companies to employ black bus drivers on routes that served black neighborhoods. Their third demand was a guarantee of courteous treatment by white drivers.

Coretta remembered that it was hard to talk that night because the phone kept ringing. It was after midnight when the Kings finally got to sleep. Less than six hours later, they were up, anxious to see if the boycott would be successful.

Just before 6:00 A.M. on December 5, Corrie walked into the living room to watch for the first bus to pass their house. It was right on time. In the morning darkness, the bus was all lit up inside, and Coretta could see clearly. She began shouting for Martin who came in and stood beside her. Not a single person was on the bus!

The couple stood in their living room and watched for the next bus to come, then the next, and the next. This was the most crowded route in all of Montgomery. On that December morning, no black person had boarded a bus. The boycott was working.

Long after the actual events, Coretta would remember the night when the boycott was officially extended until the demands of the black community were met. Because of her newborn baby, she was not able to go to the Holt Avenue Baptist Church where the first of many mass meetings was held. Martin described the crowds of people who were there.

Excited by the enthusiasm of the crowd, Martin made an inspiring speech. He urged his people to "protest courageously and with dignity" and warned them against using violence of any kind. "Our method must be persuasion, not coercion," he said. Nonviolence was to be the unique contribution of Martin Luther King's message.

Coretta, committed to peace and racial equality since her college days, fully supported her husband's ideas. She acted as an unofficial secretary for the MIA, answering the telephone in their home, which rang from dawn until midnight. All day long, groups of people were meeting in the King house.

As the boycott dragged on, the telephone calls became increasingly unpleasant. White people who were against any increased rights for black citizens tried to scare Martin and Coretta. Some just cursed and called them names. Others actually threatened to kill them.

Martin and the other ministers so inspired the black population of the city, that the boycott was ninety-five percent effective. Despite the hardship, people walked to work or organized car pools for a full year.

The bus company was losing a great deal of money, but still it refused to give in to black demands. Instead, the city government decided on a get-tough policy that included arresting Dr. King on January 26, 1956 on a false charge of speeding. Although Coretta had been warned that this would happen, it left both her and Martin shaken. Martin later told her that he had been frightened when he went to jail for the first time. In later years, being arrested or jailed would become more routine, but it was never pleasant.

The Kings continued to receive threatening telephone calls. Finally Coretta took the phone off the hook at night so they could get some sleep. Never knowing what kind of vicious attack she would hear made Coretta nervous and edgy. If she answered sharply, Martin would say, "Be nice. Be kind. Be nonviolent." Coretta believed in nonviolence as much as Martin did, but as she explained, "I was just too tired and worn out to be nonviolent."

It was not only the phone calls but the threats themselves that worried Coretta and Martin. Someone might actually try to kill them. Since the boycott had begun two months ago, Coretta and the baby were alone a great deal. Martin felt that someone should be with his family when he was away.

Although Corrie doubted that anyone would try to bomb their house, she went along with Martin's request. Mary Williams, a good friend, agreed to visit while Dr. King was speaking at the mass meeting the evening of January 30, 1956.

Yoki was asleep, and the two women were in the living room. They heard a noise on the porch as if something heavy had been thrown. As Coretta and Mary ran through the guest room toward the back of the house, they heard a deafening noise. It was followed immediately by the sound of breaking glass and the smell of smoke. They dashed into the Kings' bedroom where the baby was peacefully sleeping in her bassinet. Luckily, the blast had hit the front porch and extended only as far as the living room.

Martin was in the middle of speaking when news of the bomb reached Ralph Abernathy and others. Although they decided not to tell him until the speech was over, Martin sensed something was

Martin and Coretta being applauded by their supporters during the Montgomery bus boycott.

wrong. Then Abernathy walked up to him and gave him a note. It stated that the King house had been bombed, but no one was injured. Dr. King read it aloud and called on the hundreds of black people in the audience to remain calm. Then he quickly returned home to Coretta and their daughter, Yolanda.

When Martin arrived, a large crowd had already gathered at the house, including the mayor and white police officials. There were also white and black reporters and many angry black people. Some held guns, rocks, knives, or sticks. They were angry and shouted insults at the white police. Coretta realized that the smallest incident could start a riot.

After making sure his family was all right, Martin walked out onto the porch and held up his hand for silence. "My wife and my baby are all right," he said. "I want you to go home and put down your weapons . . . We must meet violence with nonviolence."

Even after this frightening attack on her and on their home and family, Coretta did not regret her decision. Less than two years before, she had not wanted to move to Montgomery. Now she could see a greater purpose in their decision, a purpose "much bigger than Montgomery."

Neither bombs nor other forms of intimidation made Montgomery's African-American community return to the buses until their demands were met. As the boycott continued, Martin and Coretta became famous throughout the United States among white and black people.

During the year of the boycott, Coretta sang at several concerts. One was in Chicago at a meeting of the National Baptist Convention in September 1956. While there Coretta talked about the struggles of Montgomery's black citizens.

On December 5, 1956, Coretta sang at a concert in New York City to raise money for the Montgomery Improvement Association. Besides Coretta, other performers included the famous folk singer Harry Belafonte and jazz musician Duke Ellington.

Coretta loved music. This photograph appeared on a program of one of her many recitals.

When Coretta was called to perform, she first sang several classical pieces. Then she told the story of the Montgomery movement and creatively wove familiar black spirituals and folk songs into the narrative. When the performance was over, she knew it had been a success.

The concert ended an eventful year for the Kings and for all of black America. It marked the beginning of what was to become "a worldwide struggle."

4

"Our Faith Has Now Been Vindicated"

On November 13, 1956, news of victory came to the citizens of Montgomery. The U.S. Supreme Court had ruled that Alabama's law requiring segregation on buses was unconstitutional. "Our faith has now been vindicated," Martin said in his Christmas sermon. The first of many battles had been won.

Nothing in the fight to end segregation was easy, however. Coretta was fearful as her husband joined a group of black and white citizens and boarded the first desegregated bus on December 21. That day was uneventful, but during the next few weeks buses were stoned and black peoples' homes and churches were bombed.

The success of the Montgomery boycott encouraged blacks in other cities to fight for their rights. Many of them contacted Martin before they launched their own boycotts or nonviolent campaigns. Among them were black ministers and civil rights activists. Gradually, African Americans found that they needed a central organization to mobilize the fight for equality.

After a year of discussions, a meeting was organized. The final plans were made in Martin and Coretta's living room in December 1956. A conference of black leaders would meet in Atlanta and plan strategy. It was scheduled for January 10, 1957, and tentatively called the Southern Negro Leaders Conference on Transportation and Non-Violent Integration.

Martin, Coretta, and their baby daughter arrived early so they could visit with Martin's family. Just a few hours before the proceedings were to begin, a phone call came. Two homes and four churches in Montgomery had been bombed, including the home and church of Ralph and Juanita Abernathy.

The news shocked everyone. It was a reminder that the victory in the Supreme Court was only one small battle in the civil rights war. Many whites were bitter about the progress blacks were making. They were not ready to accept what the Supreme Court said was the law.

Ralph Abernathy had come to Atlanta with Corrie and Martin to attend the meeting. Although his wife and child were unharmed, Abernathy wanted to return to Montgomery during this crisis.

Martin believed that Ralph and the people of Montgomery needed him, too. But here in Atlanta an important meeting was about to start, and he was expected to run it. Who could take over for him?

Years later Abernathy wrote that Coretta herself asked, "Can't I run the meeting for a day until you get back?" Martin agreed, and Coretta King, together with Rev. Fred Shuttlesworth, made the opening presentation.

Martin was back the next day and signed his name to letters of protest that were sent to President Eisenhower and U.S. Attorney General Herbert Brownell. A second meeting was scheduled in New Orleans, but Coretta had helped lay the groundwork in Atlanta. The new organization was named the Southern Christian Leadership Conference (SCLC).

Right after the New Orleans meeting, Martin appeared on the

cover of *Time* magazine. The article told about his leadership of the Montgomery bus boycott. And right on page twenty was a picture of Coretta and their daughter, Yolanda King. The caption read: "They earned their right to the name."

With the founding of the SCLC and Martin's inclusion in *Time*, an avalanche of activity began. Invitations poured in asking Martin to speak. People came from all over the world with offers to help the famous Dr. King.

Coretta was hospitable to everyone. She never knew how many people would appear to share their dinner on any evening. Guests "couldn't be allowed to starve," insisted Coretta.

One invitation that came for Coretta and Martin was especially exciting. On March 6, 1957, the new African country of Ghana, a former British colony, would declare its independence. Ghana was one of the first black African countries to become self-governing. Its leader, Kwame Nkrumah, was an African who had been educated in the United States. He wanted Martin Luther King, Jr., to attend the ceremonies.

Although Coretta and Martin would be the guests of the government of Ghana, they needed money to pay for airline fares and other expenses. Donations from the Dexter Avenue church and the MIA made it possible for Coretta and Martin to make the trip.

In Accra, the capital city of Ghana, Martin and Coretta witnessed the ceremony in which power passed from the British government to native African rulers. Coretta saw President Nkrumah, in his vividly colored robe, the traditional dress of his own African tribe.

As the bells struck midnight, the British flag was slowly lowered, and the flag of Ghana was raised. The African people shouted, "Freedom!" in different tribal languages. Pride in her African heritage was to remain with Coretta from the time of this event. She would also remember the poverty of the Africans, " . . . living under conditions of filth and squalor that exceeded even the worst state of Negroes in America."

After Ghana, Martin and Corrie visited Nigeria, Rome, Geneva, Paris, and London for the first time. Wherever they went they were received by dignitaries in the U.S. embassies and entertained by government officials.

Back in Montgomery, Martin and Coretta were thrust into renewed civil rights activities. The SCLC was planning a major march on Washington, D.C. Its purpose was to urge the passage of the new civil rights bill guaranteeing all African Americans the right to vote. The bill outlawed local practices such as poll taxes or complicated literacy tests. These were used in the South to prevent black people from registering to vote.

American blacks also wanted to show their unity and give white northerners a chance to join and support their cause. A large crowd in Washington, D.C., might win President Eisenhower's public support. Martin wanted the president to speak with black leaders and encourage the new civil rights legislation.

In order to stress the nonviolent nature of this demonstration, Martin called the march a Prayer Pilgrimage for Freedom. Coretta was pregnant with their second child but hoped to participate since it involved less than a mile walk. Martin indicated, however, that he expected her to be at home. Twelve years later she wrote matter-of-factly, "Because of my pregnancy I was unable to go, which I deeply regretted."

People in the SCLC remembered Coretta's pleasant disposition in the face of disappointment. She always remained loyal to her husband even when she disagreed with his decisions. Rarely did she allow anyone to suspect her personal dissatisfaction.

Although the turnout at the Prayer Pilgrimage was less than the hoped-for 50,000, Martin's first speech to a national audience made headlines. On the radio, Coretta listened as Martin urged: "Give us the ballot and . . . we will write the proper laws on the books."

After his national radio and television appearance, Martin received more invitations than ever. In addition to speeches, he began writing his first book, *Stride Toward Freedom*, the story of the Montgomery bus boycott. This again meant time away from Coretta and Yoki.

In spite of a busy schedule, Martin was home on October 23, 1957, when their first son was born. Corrie herself had misgivings

Martin Luther King, III, was born in 1957. Here he is shown at six weeks old, with his sister Yolanda.

about naming boys after their fathers, but once again she gave in to her husband and named their son Martin Luther King III.

Having two young children kept Corrie at home during 1957 and 1958. For much of that time, Martin was away, busy with meetings, out-of-town speeches, and demands by supporters.

In an interview with *Life* magazine, Coretta admitted, "Frankly I worry about him. He never has a minute to himself. When he isn't in court, he is attending meetings of the MIA. When he's home, he's always on the phone. People call him from all over the country."

Only a hint of Coretta's loneliness and discontent can be sensed in her subsequent words to the interviewer. "I try to protect him as much as possible, so that he can rest, but there is little that I can do."

5

"Lord, I Hope This Isn't the Way Martin Has to Go"

Because Coretta understood the importance of her husband's work, it was difficult to complain. Martin would come home from a trip, make twenty or more long-distance calls, and then rush off to another meeting. By the time the meeting was over, the children had been asleep for hours, and both Martin and Coretta were tired.

All his civil rights activities plus his pastoral work filled Martin's days and nights. He wished for more time with his wife and children, but other issues pulled him away. When finally his first book, *Stride Toward Freedom*, was completed, he and Corrie went to Mexico.

Even on vacation, the extreme differences between rich and poor distressed Coretta and Martin. They could not forget their commitment to fight against poverty and injustice. These two weeks away helped the Kings relax and become reacquainted with each other, but when they returned home, the daily pressures of work and worry were still present.

One incident occurred at the entrance to the courthouse in

Montgomery. It served as a reminder of how much needed to be done to improve the lives of black people. Ralph Abernathy was scheduled to testify in court, and Martin and Coretta came to be with him and watch the trial. When they got to the door, a white policeman prevented them from entering. He was especially insulting to Martin and addressed him as "Boy."

The word "boy" was often used in the South by whites when talking to black men. It implied that, even when fully grown and educated, African-American men were really like children and not worthy of respect. To address a man of Martin's stature as "Boy," meant that the policeman had no regard for him. Dr. King was a minister with a Ph.D. degree, but the white police saw only his black skin.

Martin was arrested for loitering, a word that means hanging around or lingering aimlessly. A trial was set for a few days later. The Kings and their friends understood that charges like these were meant to frighten Martin and his associates and stop them from working for equal rights.

When Martin's trial came up and he was fined ten dollars, he refused to pay. The authorities were surprised and confused. They did not really want him in jail. Montgomery already had too much bad publicity, and the officials preferred to forget it. Martin insisted on waiting at the courthouse to be taken to jail.

Finally the judge told him someone had paid the fine and he had to go home. That "someone" was the police commissioner, Clyde Sellers, who did not wish to give Dr. King any more publicity.

In September 1958, *Stride Toward Freedom*, the story of the Montgomery bus boycott, was published. The publishers arranged a series of lectures around the country, so Dr. King could introduce his new book.

Early in the tour, Martin was scheduled for several appearances in New York City. One of them was at Blumstein's department store in Harlem, a large black neighborhood.

Martin was seated in the store, autographing copies of his book, and surrounded by admirers. A middle-aged black woman approached and asked, "Is this Martin Luther King?" Martin looked up and answered, "Yes, it is." Hearing that, the woman took out a sharp letter opener and stabbed him in the chest.

Coretta was expecting her husband to return that evening and was planning to pick him up at the airport. Instead she received a phone call telling her that Martin had been hurt. He had been attacked by "an obviously deranged" woman and was in the hospital.

"Lord, I hope this is not the way Martin has to go," Corrie sobbed. She immediately arranged to fly to New York. In spite of recurrent nightmares about Martin getting injured or killed, she was unprepared for this crisis.

Only after she arrived at the hospital did Coretta learn how close to death her husband had been. The tip of the letter opener had been so close to his heart that if Martin had sneezed or moved suddenly, he would have died. He had undergone surgery and was still in critical condition when Coretta was allowed in to see him.

When she saw that Martin would be all right, Coretta calmed down. Together with the SCLC executive director, she set up a temporary office in space provided for them at Harlem Hospital. They worked night and day responding to thousands of well-wishers and keeping track of the contributions that poured in.

Three weeks later, Martin returned to Montgomery to rest and regain his strength. Coretta again took her husband's place for an important event. The Youth March for Integrated Schools was already scheduled for October 25 in Washington, D.C. Coretta, along with Harry Belafonte, Jackie Robinson, the first black baseball star, and A. Philip Randolph, the head of the Brotherhood of Sleeping Car Porters, an important black labor union, led the march. Before an audience of 10,000 people, mostly college students, Coretta delivered Martin's written speech.

Coretta remembered the weeks of Martin's recovery as a relatively peaceful period. Because he was not traveling for the civil rights movement, this seemed to be a good time to accept an invitation to visit India.

For Martin, the invitation was very special. It had come from the Gandhi National Memorial Fund. Mohandas Gandhi was an Indian nationalist who developed the method of nonviolent protest that Martin Luther King admired. Some people had compared the Montgomery bus boycott to Gandhi's protest marches against English rule in India. Money from a U.S. foundation made it possible for Corrie and Martin to make the trip.

Neither Coretta nor Martin was prepared for the kind of poverty that existed in India. They saw many people dressed in rags and begging. Some had no permanent shelter and slept on the streets. In contrast to this poverty, the Kings were received by Prime Minister Jawaharlal Nehru in his elegant home.

In India Coretta and Martin learned more about Gandhi's ideas and about other eastern philosophies. They saw what it meant to live simply, with few possessions, and realized how much patience it took to begin a real revolution. Coming back to the United States, they tried to incorporate these ideas into their own lives.

"You know, a man who dedicates himself to a cause doesn't need a family," Martin told Coretta after the trip.

Coretta insisted that she "was not hurt by this statement." She understood that Martin loved his family as always but that his life would be devoted to the movement.

Martin was soon on the road again, making speeches. In spite of his family's needs, he chose to give almost all his speaking fees to the SCLC. The civil rights movement needed it to pay salaries, rent, and other expenses. Martin did not want a bigger house or a fancy car.

Even with Martin's sacrifices, the SCLC was at a low point in 1959. Funds were short, and leadership and morale had suffered. The goal of registering black voters throughout the South was far behind. Black activists were becoming restless.

The King family having a family dinner together. The Kings kept a portrait on their wall of Mohandas Gandhi, a person whose ideas they admired greatly.

Martin made an important decision. He would give up being pastor at the Dexter Avenue Baptist Church, return to Atlanta, and devote himself to the civil rights movement.

Daddy King had been urging Martin and Coretta to come back since the first bombing of their home. At first Coretta and Martin refused because of their important work in Montgomery. But now the Montgomery bus boycott had ended successfully, and the civil rights movement was changing. Coretta and Martin had to be prepared to change, too.

Martin's father was happy about the prospect of having his son and his family back home. The Ebenezer Baptist Church, where Daddy King had been pastor for so many years, offered Martin a position as co-pastor. The salary was $4,200 per year, hardly enough for a growing family. Still, the job offered Martin the time he needed to devote himself to civil rights.

When necessary, Martin added to this salary from his speaking fees. That first year, he earned $230,000 speaking for the SCLC. Only $5,000 was used for personal needs. The rest went to support the movement.

Because of Martin's attitudes about money and personal possessions, it distressed Coretta to know that many SCLC supporters were attacking her husband. They blamed him for his misuse of the organization's money. When the state of Alabama accused Martin of falsifying his income tax returns, it seemed especially unfair.

Coretta knew that Martin did not take any of the movement funds for his personal use. She understood that he was ready to give his life for the cause of civil rights. When the verdict of "not guilty" was handed down by an all-white Alabama jury, Coretta was overjoyed.

That same night, Coretta flew to Cleveland. She had been invited to speak at the Antioch Baptist Church Women's Day. Instead of reading her prepared speech, Coretta told the audience about the events of her life and the courtroom drama in Montgomery. She had the impression that the women understood what she said.

Coretta's successes in public speaking gave her more confidence. She was beginning to develop her own interests and accomplishments outside her home and family. In 1957 the National Council of Negro Women gave her their annual Brotherhood Award. Coretta was grateful that, through concerts and speeches, she could also contribute to the cause.

Another of Coretta's long-standing interests was her commitment to world peace. When the Kings moved to Atlanta, she became a member of the Women's International League for Peace and Freedom. According to Alice Walker, a black author who met Mrs. King early in the 1960s, Coretta "seemed to be the only black woman in Atlanta actively and publicly engaged in the pursuit of peace." Ms. Walker remembers Coretta at that time as "bright-eyed, slim and bubbly . . . her long hair tied back in a simple, slightly curly ponytail."

Coretta had always believed that the concern for world peace and the fight for civil rights were one struggle. At Antioch College she had belonged to the NAACP, the Council on Race Relations, and peace groups. Later, this commitment to peace would become stronger, but in 1960 Coretta had many family responsibilities.

Ten years later, in an interview, she confessed that she and her husband regularly discussed her outside involvements. "We always agreed that when both of us were under a lot of pressure to be away from home, I would be the one to curtail my activities . . . I wasn't too unhappy about this," admitted Coretta. "My top priority has always been my family."

By mid-1961, Coretta was pregnant with her third child. Fear for Martin and his safety had become a part of the reality of her busy and demanding life. But Corrie would have to draw on all of her strength and faith to cope with what lay ahead.

6

"Everything We Can to Help"

Boycotts and protests became a part of life in the South. In 1960 college students began sit-ins, a method of trying to integrate lunch counters.

Similar sit-ins had been attempted before this, but the press had never reported the story on a national scale. Then in 1960, when students began doing the same thing in Greensboro, North Carolina, more people became involved. Dr. King was invited to talk to the students about nonviolence, and from this beginning a new civil rights organization was formed: the Student Nonviolent Coordinating Committee (SNCC).

The formation of the SNCC added to deepening divisions among the civil rights activists. There was a general distrust of the young protesters by many older SLC members. In spite of this, Martin became more involved with this new student-run group. He joined in the sit-ins and as a result was jailed several times. Usually Martin was released immediately, but once he was held longer.

"Why does Daddy have to go to jail?" five-year-old Yoki asked Coretta. It was difficult to explain that to little children. Jail was usually associated with punishment for doing something wrong.

Coretta knew that this was not true for Martin. She decided on an honest but simple answer while the children were still so young. "Daddy goes to jail to help people," she told them.

This new stay in jail was the result of a minor event that happened many months before. While bringing a white friend home, Martin was stopped for driving with an expired Alabama license. A charge like that does not usually result in being arrested and taken to jail. Martin, however, was a black man who had been "making trouble" for whites in the South. Because of this, the police were always ready to arrest him. It was an excuse to discourage him from his work. Martin was arrested for not having a proper driver's license and then released on probation.

When he was subsequently arrested for the sit-in in Atlanta, the Alabama police requested that Dr. King be returned to that state to be tried. They claimed he had violated his probation by participating in the sit-in. It was not a surprise when the Alabama judge found Martin guilty. But what came next *was* a surprise. Martin was sentenced to four months in jail at hard labor.

Coretta was shocked. Four months in jail for a traffic violation! Martin's sister Christine began crying, and Coretta suddenly broke down, too. She was due to deliver their third child in just a few months and felt alone and helpless. What would happen to her husband after four months in a white jail?

When she was allowed in to see Martin, Coretta tried to control the tears, but it was impossible. "You have to be strong for me," Martin urged her.

Hearing Martin's voice she suddenly realized what *he* was going through. Martin had already spent eight days in jail. He was alone, tired, and frightened.

So many times before this Coretta had explained to Yoki and Marty why their Daddy had to go to jail. "To help other people," she told them again and again. But this time was different. Coretta left the jailhouse feeling panicked. She called lawyer Harris

Wofford and sobbed into the phone: "They are going to kill him. I know they are going to kill him."

Returning home, Coretta King collected some newspapers and writing material for Martin to use while in prison. The next day she was preparing to meet with Wofford, who was already working for Martin's release, when suddenly the phone rang.

The voice on the other end of the telephone spoke. "Just a minute, Mrs. King, for Senator Kennedy."

Senator John F. Kennedy was running for president of the United States. Just days before the election he had heard of this latest injustice against Dr. King. "I understand you are expecting a baby," said the senator. "I just wanted to let you know that I am concerned and that we are going to do everything we can to help." He told Mrs. King to feel free to call on him.

Coretta was not sure how to react to a call from this famous man. She did not know whether he could really help Martin but soon found that he could. A few phone calls from important people had caused the judge to change his mind. Within one day, Martin was released from jail.

Later that week, on November 8, 1960, John F. Kennedy was elected president of the United States. Coretta is still convinced that his concern and help for her husband was what gave him those extra votes to win.

With a sympathetic president in the White House, the civil rights movement seemed to take off. Expert fund-raisers in New York added to the SCLC's regular income from Martin's speeches. Sit-ins became bigger, and college students from the North, both white and black, organized. Busloads of people traveled together into southern states to force an end to segregation. Their goal was to remove the "whites only" signs from southern restaurants, bus stations, and public facilities.

These people, committed to equal justice for Negroes, as African Americans were called in 1960, were known as Freedom

Riders. The Freedom Riders came down in groups on public interstate buses. They refused to obey the signs segregating the races in bus depots and lunch counters.

Southern whites who opposed desegregation often resorted to violence. Buses were attacked with rocks, guns, and bombs. Riders were beaten up, threatened, sometimes even killed. Martin spoke to the Freedom Riders but never actually rode a bus with them. His failure to do this was resented by the student activists for a long time.

Coretta could only watch these activities on television. She was busy with her new baby, Dexter, born in January 1961 and could not participate in all these events.

Although Martin faced many difficulties, Corrie had problems of her own and could not help resenting her husband's absences. It was not easy to be the wife of a great leader. Coretta was always proud of him, and the children adored him, but he was rarely there when his family needed him.

A world-renowned public figure may not always make the best husband and father. Even though Martin loved his family, he was distant from daily decisions. When Coretta wanted to choose a school for their oldest child, Yoki, who was beginning first grade, Martin told her he would leave it up to her.

Since their trip to India, Martin was even less concerned with material things than he had once been. Coretta wanted to move from their old rented house on Johnson Avenue into a larger place. She believed that with their growing family they needed the extra room. However, Martin resisted owning anything that was not essential for the children.

As the civil rights movement continued growing, decisions such as schools for the children and a new house were pushed further aside. In 1955 Coretta had written to a friend at the New England Conservatory of Music, "It has seemed . . . at times there should have been at least three of me." This was even more true in 1961 with a family of three young children.

Each new project that Martin took on meant increased work for Coretta and, of course, more time alone. A newspaper article described Coretta's job as "organizing behind the scenes, tending . . . small children [and] fielding death threats from rednecks . . ." (Redneck was an expression once used to describe white segregationist men in the South.)

Early in 1962 Martin was invited to join the drive to end segregation in Albany, Georgia, a small city near Atlanta. The Albany protest had been launched by the Student Nonviolent Coordinating Committee and local black leaders in December 1961. Now they needed Martin's help.

The Albany protest was not successful. There was constant disagreement among the various black organizations involved. The white segregationists sensed this and refused to give in. Martin was sent to jail several times for leading demonstrations or prayer vigils.

During one of Martin's imprisonments, Coretta brought her two older children, Yoki and Marty, to see their father in jail. Because they were so young, the police chief allowed Martin to visit with them out in the corridor where they played happily.

When Martin's trial date arrived, Coretta fully expected him to be sentenced to more time in jail. In order to keep the protest going, Coretta and Juanita Abernathy spoke at a rally in Albany at Shiloh Baptist Church. Since both their husbands were in jail, the two women planned to lead a new march. They would be joined by the wives of all the other jailed civil rights leaders.

Planning this march was challenging for Coretta, but it was never actually carried out. Martin and Ralph were given suspended sentences and released. Since there was no longer a need to protest, the plans for a march were cancelled. Coretta admitted that she was disappointed.

In her autobiography Coretta explained that she felt her

participation in the civil rights movement was not complete because she did not go to jail. She longed to be actively involved and grasped every opportunity to participate.

Whether it was a concert, a rally, or a speech, Coretta was always ready. While she accepted Martin's belief that the children needed her, there were still times when she could get away. Sometimes their differing attitudes about Corrie's involvement in the movement's work led to arguments.

Once or twice Coretta even asked a friend to convince Martin to allow her a more active role. Martin did not accept these suggestions kindly. He never really stopped believing that his wife's place was at home.

In spite of her husband's attitude, Coretta did manage to participate in many activities. One of the most memorable was when she was invited to be a delegate for Women's Strike for Peace. She was one of only four African Americans in the delegation. The group of fifty American women would attend the 17-nation General Disarmament Conference in 1962 in Geneva, Switzerland. Coretta was very anxious to go, and this time Martin encouraged her.

In Geneva, the delegation met with United States and Russian representatives and tried to influence the policy-making groups who were discussing a treaty to ban atomic bomb testing. Coretta always believed that "the women of the world . . . can become a most powerful force for international peace . . ."

Although no major change came out of this international meeting, Coretta was impressed with the women involved. She became even more committed to peace. After the conference, Coretta returned to Atlanta and resumed her role at home. Before very long the Kings were expecting their fourth child.

Martin had recently met a lawyer from New York named Harry Wachtel. He was anxious to help the cause of civil rights in any way that he could, and he and Martin became good friends.

Harry remembered the first time he met Corrie at her home in

Atlanta. "She was a very attractive person," he said. Wachtel recalled that Coretta controlled her children very carefully and was deferential (respectful) to her husband. During that visit at least, "she stayed in the background."

Martin and the SCLC were now involved in a new project in Birmingham, Alabama. Rev. Fred Shuttlesworth first organized this drive against segregation in 1962.

Elected officials in Alabama spent all their energy trying to resist any changes proposed by civil rights groups. In November 1962 George Wallace was elected governor of Alabama with a promise of "segregation forever." In the city of Birmingham the commissioner of public safety, Eugene "Bull" Connor, was also committed to segregation.

Martin wanted to prevent another failure like the one at Albany. Plans for the protest were carefully organized, and a schedule was set up before Martin officially entered Birmingham.

Coretta worried that their fourth child would be born while Martin was away, but he was in Atlanta on March 28, 1963, the day Bernice Albertine—nicknamed Bunny—was born. The next day he left for Birmingham, rushed back a week later to bring Coretta home with the new baby, and returned to Birmingham the same night. When he left Coretta at home, both of them knew that, because of the protest marches, Martin would be in jail in a few days.

7

"Watch It, Man, That's Mrs. King"

As Coretta had expected, it was not long before her husband was arrested again. It was nearing Easter weekend. Martin knew that if he led another march in Birmingham, he could be in jail for the entire holiday. Even though it meant being away from his family, Martin decided to go ahead. He believed that it was necessary for the movement and that his arrest at this time would have moral significance.

Corrie got word from Birmingham that Martin, along with Ralph Abernathy and many other black leaders, had been taken to jail. She waited for his call, "always the first thing he did after he was arrested." But this time there was no call.

Throughout the weekend Coretta waited. Desperate and worried, she telephoned Wyatt Walker, one of Martin's assistants, to find out what was happening. He explained that Martin was not allowed to see or talk with anyone, not even his lawyers.

Walker had a daring idea. "I think you should call the president," he said.

It seemed like a big decision to make alone, and she wanted to talk it over with her husband. Walker tried to contact Martin, but it was impossible. Coretta had no choice but to go ahead without his approval.

Getting the call through to the White House was complicated. Everyone was out of the capital on this holiday weekend. Finally, a helpful telephone operator put Coretta through to Pierre Salinger, President Kennedy's press secretary. Through his intervention, Coretta received a call from the president's brother, Robert Kennedy, who was U.S. attorney general.

Coretta explained the problem to Robert Kennedy and stressed that she did not want to get her husband out of jail—she knew he would not want that. She only wanted to make sure he was all right and to speak with him.

The attorney general explained the problems from his end but promised Coretta he would "look into the situation and let you know something."

Robert Kennedy kept his word. On Monday, the president himself called Coretta, and they chatted like old friends. Then President Kennedy told her he had spoken with officials in Birmingham, and Martin would be calling her soon. The conversation ended with the assurance that Coretta could call the president or his brother whenever she needed to.

Sure enough, less than one half hour after she spoke with the president, Martin called. A few days later he was released but not before writing what became one of the most famous documents of the civil rights movement: the "Letter from the Birmingham Jail."

Martin's letter was an answer to a group of white Alabama clergymen who had accused him of being an "outside agitator." Martin defended his presence on religious and moral grounds. He wrote, "I am in Birmingham because injustice is here."

Sent from jail, Martin's letter was published in newspapers throughout the country. It made him and the civil rights movement even more well known and respected by people who believed in fairness and justice.

Unfair laws were effectively enforced in Birmingham by the segregationists. But ultimately, they could not hold out against the commitment of people who were willing to go to jail, to be beaten, or to die for the cause. In Birmingham, even young children were beaten and jailed. The police assaulted the peaceful demonstrators with water hoses and with dogs. The marchers did not resist but each day returned to demonstrate for equal rights.

Finally, the Alabama police could no longer obey their chief's orders. The marchers, many of them young people from grade school and high school, were allowed through to the capitol to hold a prayer vigil.

With the help of federal mediators, a settlement was reached

In 1963, Attorney General Robert Kennedy helped Coretta when Martin was imprisoned in Birmingham. Here, she speaks with him many years later.

between black and white citizens in Birmingham. Stores were to be desegregated, more African Americans would be hired, and an interracial council organized.

Coretta later wrote about Birmingham: ". . . black people had never acted along such a broad front . . . to alter the conditions of their lives." As a result of this success President Kennedy decided to propose a civil rights bill to Congress for 1963.

The victory celebration was brief. One day after Martin returned to Atlanta, black homes in Birmingham were bombed. Outraged black people took to the streets and began to riot. Although Martin managed to rush back and calm the city, resistance to integration was far from over.

Bombings erupted repeatedly in this and other cities across the South. Martin's enemies were quietly looking for new ways to discredit him and the movement he represented.

In spite of threats, real fears for himself and his family, and the tensions of leadership, Martin continued his work. He could not let the momentum toward equal rights slow down. Coretta advised Martin to work on another march on Washington for legislation to help black people.

As with so many ideas, this one also came from several people at the same time. Some historians credited A. Philip Randolph, head of the Brotherhood of Sleeping Car Porters, with the proposal for the march. But whoever initiated the plan, responsibility for this major event was shared among all the black leadership. White leaders also joined in this effort to appeal to Congress and the nation for passage of the President's civil rights bill.

The march was scheduled for August 28, 1963, and this time Coretta, too, would be participating. However, she would not be able to march with her husband. It had been decided that the march would be led by the top leadership only.

Coretta acceded to the wishes of the leaders but later wrote that she felt the decision was unfair. The wives "had shared the dangers and hardships" of the movement, and they should have been allowed to march with their husbands, Coretta believed.

Coretta had also wanted to go with Martin to the White House after the march, when he and other black leaders had been invited to speak with President Kennedy. Martin refused, explaining that it was not customary for leaders to bring their wives to meetings with the president.

The day of the march, Coretta was there with Martin, eager to

White segregationists did not want to see civil rights laws passed. Some bombed homes owned by blacks.

participate in any way she could. It was exciting to stand at the window of their hotel room, to watch the crowd of 250,000 people gathering, and to listen to the television reports. Coretta marched with Ralph and Juanita Abernathy, Wyatt Walker, Dr. Ralph Bunche, former ambassador to the United Nations, and several other famous African Americans. She did manage to get a seat on the platform almost directly behind Martin.

Coretta had shared her husband's concerns about this march and its goals. She had been with him in the hotel room when he wrote his speech, struggling for just the right words. Now she was hearing something different. Somewhere in the middle of his talk, with the crowd hanging on his words and repeating them after him, Martin looked up from the written text and began to speak spontaneously, from his heart.

"I have a dream," he shouted out to the crowds, "that one day . . . the sons of former slaves and the sons of former slaveowners will be able to sit down together at the table of brotherhood."

Martin Luther King, Jr., in a speech that has since been quoted hundreds of times, spoke on. He told the nation about his dreams of freedom, "when all God's children, black men and white men, Jews and Gentiles, Protestants and Catholics, will be able to join hands and sing . . . 'Free at last!' "

When the speech was over, Coretta was filled with pride. U.S. marshals came over and made a circle around her husband to protect him from the emotional mobs who tried to reach out and touch him. Coretta got up from her chair and put her arm through Martin's. She clung to him as he was propelled off the stand and away from the crowd. As one of the marshals pulled at her, she heard another say: "Watch it, man, that's Mrs. King."

The march on Washington in 1963 was one of the high points of the year for Coretta. It was followed by tragedies, one right after another. The first, on September 15, was the bombing of a black church in Birmingham. Four little girls attending Sunday school were killed in the blast. Just two months later, on November 22, President Kennedy was gunned down during a motorcade in Dallas, Texas, and died.

Six years later, Coretta recalled how deeply affected she was. Kennedy had been not only the president but a "kind and thoughtful . . . friend."

The King children, as young as they were, were also saddened when they heard about the president's death. Yoki, just eight years old, only dimly understood the significance of the assassination, but she worried aloud, ". . . we're never going to get our freedom now."

Martin's reaction was a more personal one. "This is what is going to happen to me also," he said to Coretta. Coretta had no answer for her husband. She sat beside him and held his hand.

The new year, 1964, began with new tragedy. The bodies of three civil rights activists—two whites and one black—were found in a local dam in Mississippi. County Sheriff Rainey and his deputy were believed responsible. Martin gave the eulogy at the memorial service for the three young men, James Chaney, Andrew Goodman, and Michael Schwerner.

One great success in 1964, however, was the Civil Rights Act, passed by Congress and signed by President Lyndon B. Johnson. The act included a public accommodations bill, outlawing segregated public facilities in the United States. Martin was at the White House for the signing on July 2.

Coretta began a new series of concerts in 1964 to raise money for new civil rights goals. In songs and words, she told of the ongoing struggle of African Americans for freedom.

Coretta was proud of the money she raised. In the first concert, presented at Town Hall in New York, her efforts brought in $6,000. The proceeds were divided between the SCLC and the Goodman-Chaney-Schwerner Fund, a civil rights fund organized by the fathers of the three young men who were killed in Alabama.

Martin was doubtful about Coretta's attempts at fund-raising. When the Freedom Concerts contributed more than $50,000 for the SCLC, he had to admit he was wrong.

Fatigue and tension pursued Martin and Coretta wherever they went. When the civil rights killings abated, the personal death threats against Martin and his family still continued. Although Coretta claimed she was getting used to them, they took a toll on the family.

One night some men came and burned a cross on the Kings' lawn while Martin was away. Burning a cross was the traditional warning issued by the Ku Klux Klan, a white supremacist organization in the South that often killed blacks. Coretta insisted she was not afraid.

For Martin, the strain was even worse than for Coretta. In addition to his white segregationist enemies, he now found there were others who sought to discredit him and cause his downfall. One of those people was J. Edgar Hoover, head of the Federal Bureau of Investigation (FBI).

Mr. Hoover first became aware of Martin Luther King, Jr., during the early civil rights movement. Because some of Martin's close associates, including lawyer Stanley Levison, were accused of being communists, Hoover ordered a tap on Martin's telephone.

Telephone taps and surveillance did not reveal any communist plots. They appeared to reveal that Martin was involved in activities that many people considered immoral, especially for a married man and a Baptist minister. It was alleged that, unknown to Coretta, Martin Luther King had several relationships with other women while he was away from home.

Soon the FBI was actively pursuing Dr. King, trying to expose these private indiscretions. Some of his associates believed that women were Martin's weakness. In spite of the real dangers to his reputation, Martin seemed unable to change.

Added to all the other stresses in his life, this new problem was upsetting to Martin. In an attempt to overcome the depression and exhaustion, he checked into a hospital for a complete rest. It was during this hospital stay that Coretta got a call from the Associated Press. Her husband had won the Nobel Peace Prize.

Once the news spread, Martin could get no rest. Coretta, conceding that "this was exactly the sort of lift Martin desperately needed," did not try to protect him from reporters or the hundreds of well-wishers who flocked to his hospital room.

Very quickly, plans were under way for the trip to Oslo, Norway, where Martin would receive the prize and the money— $54,000. It would all go to the movement, Martin insisted.

Coretta believed that some of the prize money should be used for the family, specifically, $5,000 for each of their children's educations. Martin was adamant that he would only use the money for the cause of civil rights. His wife had no choice but to go along.

Money for transportation was raised by other ministers through their churches and from special funds. Martin's family, Coretta's parents, and some of their closest friends, including the Abernathys and the Wachtels, left for London on December 4, 1964. There, Martin preached a sermon at St. Paul's Cathedral. On December 8, the King party, some thirty people, continued on to Oslo.

At the formal presentation of the prize at Oslo University, Coretta looked lovely in a fitted evening gown and long white gloves. Martin was dressed in traditional formal suit, striped trousers, a tailcoat, and an ascot tie.

Coretta admitted that she felt so proud that "I feel as if I might burst." Nothing could spoil the specialness of this week—not Martin's depression, not the difficult battles waiting at home.

From Norway the group traveled to Stockholm, Sweden. One of the highlights of their stay in this city was a grand ball, given by African students from Kenya. They insisted that Martin and Coretta honor them by dancing the first dance. Because Baptist ministers—

and their wives—usually did not dance, Coretta especially enjoyed this opportunity.

The Kings and their party went on to Paris and then back to the United States, where they received a personal welcome from President Johnson. This time, Coretta and Martin's parents were with him as they were ushered into the White House for an informal conversation with the president.

Coretta later told researchers that "only Martin's family and close staff knew how depressed he was during the entire Nobel trip." He was nervous and worried about their upcoming struggle in Selma, Alabama, and rumors surrounding the FBI wiretap.

Several months later, with Martin heavily involved in the voting rights battle in Selma, Coretta was made aware of just how dangerous the FBI could be to her husband. She received a tape in the mail, along with a threatening letter addressed to Dr. M. L. King. The tape was muffled and unclear, but it was undoubtedly Martin's voice and the voice of a woman.

The FBI's tactics frightened Coretta. Later she laughed off the incident, saying she "couldn't make much out of it. It was a lot of mumbo jumbo." She insisted that "during our whole marriage we never had one single serious discussion about either of us being involved with another person . . . all that other business just didn't have a place in the very high-level relationship we enjoyed."

Martin's reaction to this hint of scandal was very different. He maintained that "the most intimate details of [his] personal life ought to be no business of the FBI's. What I do is only between me and my God."

Friends later alluded to Martin's "compelling needs" and his constant anxiety. Coretta passed on the tapes to the SCLC and put it out of her mind. If she had any hurt or resentment, she never admitted discussing it with her husband.

8

"I Have to Resist Worry"

Martin Luther King "has been stabbed in the chest, and physically attacked three more times; his home has been bombed three times, and he has been pitched into jail fourteen times."

Chosen by *Time* as "Man of the Year" for 1964, this was just a small part of a feature story about Martin. Coretta was mentioned only briefly in the article. But it was she, too, who had to live with the repeated assaults and threats on her husband's life.

Coretta was the parent who dealt with all the family crises. On the day that President Lyndon Johnson signed the Civil Rights Act of 1964, Martin was in Washington at the ceremony. Coretta was in an Atlanta hospital where she had taken Marty and Dexter to have their tonsils removed. Martin forgot to call and find out about the children. Although Coretta recognized the enormous significance of the signing of the Civil Rights Act, she was angry at her husband's neglect of the family.

Martin was preoccupied with plans for a major voter registration drive in Selma, Alabama. However, he did attend the first integrated banquet in Atlanta in his honor. Coretta and the three older children joined him at the Dinkler Plaza Hotel where 1,500 people filled the ballroom. The Kings were seated as honored guests next to the mayor.

Four years earlier, Coretta and Martin could not even eat together with whites at a lunch counter. Tonight, blacks and whites were seated at a dinner party honoring a black leader. They joined hands and sang "We Shall Overcome." After this landmark event, Martin returned immediately to Selma.

Most people outside of Alabama had never even heard of Selma. Then Martin launched his voter registration drive there, in the heart of what was called Alabama's "black belt." White officials purposely made it difficult for black people to register in Selma. The smallest error on the long registration form might cause the applicant to be rejected—if he or she happened to be an African American.

As expected, Martin and Ralph were soon jailed in Selma for disobeying court orders that forbid them to march. Refusing bail, the two civil rights leaders made decisions, issued orders, and encouraged the protesters from their jail cell.

Andrew Young, who would later become mayor of Atlanta, worked hard to help Dr. King during this time. When he heard that Malcolm X, a controversial black leader from New York, was speaking in Selma, he quickly told Coretta to come. With Martin in jail, Andy thought she would be able to calm the crowds and prevent riots.

Coretta was reluctant, but she agreed. After her speech she met Malcolm X and was impressed with him. When he was killed two and a half weeks later, Coretta was saddened. "What a waste!" she thought.

Finally Martin was released from jail, and the campaign continued. In spite of an order from the governor prohibiting it, a long march from Selma to Montgomery, Alabama's state capital, was planned. Martin and Ralph, following SCLC policy, did not lead this march. The leadership believed that Dr. King should be available and not have to go to jail once again. He was due at the White House for a meeting with President Johnson.

As the marchers set out from Selma on Sunday, March 7, 1965, and crossed the Edmund Pettus Bridge, they were ordered to turn back. When they stopped to pray, state troopers attacked them with clubs, whips, and tear gas.

The American people watched this attack on television; white police against peaceful demonstrators. They were horrified and angry. As a result, many fair-minded white men and women from the North and the South started to support the Selma protest actively.

During the attack on the marchers, Coretta was in San Francisco. She had just finished one more of her Freedom Concerts to raise money for the SCLC, when Martin called her. He would return to Selma and lead another march himself, in spite of threats against his life.

"I have to resist worry," Coretta told herself. She knew what they were doing was right and refused to be intimidated. Despite her brave words Coretta was terribly anxious, not only about her husband but also about the children. A second march in Selma, led by Martin himself, was quickly organized. It was joined by over 1,500 people, both black and white. Once again state troopers ordered the demonstrators to halt.

This time Martin decided to stop the march and lead the people back to town rather than risk another bloody confrontation. However, even this careful obedience to the laws of southern white officials did not prevent further violence.

The senseless killing of a white minister, James Reeb, who had come to Selma to join with the civil rights marchers, moved President Johnson to make a public statement. On March 15, 1965, speaking before a joint session of Congress, the President urged passage of a new bill insuring voting rights for all people. At the end of his speech the president spoke the words that had become the rallying cry of blacks throughout the United States: "We shall overcome!" Shortly afterward, a federal court ruled that the Selma to Montgomery march was legal. Sympathizers poured into Selma.

On Sunday, March 21, Martin Luther King and Ralph Abernathy again walked over the Pettus Bridge. This time they led 3,200 marchers, including many white clergymen from the North, groups of nuns, famous entertainers, and politicians.

Coretta had a commitment to speak in North Carolina and regretted not being able to begin the march with her husband. Martin reassured her that she could join them the next day.

On Monday, Coretta marched along with the protesters, following the now famous Highway 80 toward Montgomery. Wednesday evening, together with the small group that had walked the entire way, they camped outside the city.

Coretta joined Martin in the march from Selma to Montgomery, Alabama. Thousands of civil rights supporters participated.

On Thursday, the final day of the march, thousands of people arrived from all over the country. Volunteers came by bus, train, plane, and full cars, eager to walk the final two miles. Coretta was beside Martin on this day of triumph. With pride and determination they marched through the black section of town, past the Dexter Avenue Baptist Church, where all this had begun. Along the streets, crowds of people watched and cheered them on.

It had been ten years since the Montgomery bus boycott! Coretta realized how much had changed over the years. Transportation had been desegregated, blacks could use public accommodations, and schools were being integrated.

All the marchers left Montgomery feeling optimistic. Many had already returned home when the news came that Viola Liuzzo, a white woman from Michigan and a mother of four, was killed. She was shot by Ku Klux Klansmen while driving some black volunteers back to their homes.

The Voting Rights Bill was signed into law by the president on August 6, 1965, an important step toward equality for blacks. However, Coretta realized only too well how much more there was to accomplish before African Americans would stand equal to whites.

The very next month, Coretta faced another challenge in the struggle for freedom: She registered her children in a formerly all-white school. In September 1965 Yoki and Marty, together with the three Abernathy children, became the first black students to peacefully desegregate a public school in Atlanta.

Events were less peaceful in other places. Protests for civil rights, although centered in the South, had an effect on communities throughout the United States. For the first time since Martin Luther King had begun his program for nonviolent change, northern blacks also began making demands, protesting, and sometimes rioting. Black people living in northern cities were not prevented from voting and did not ride segregated buses, but they faced major problems, also.

Black people in the United States suffered not only from poverty and prejudice. Political systems that were not responsive to the poor did nothing to help African-American citizens. They were poorer than most whites and had fewer opportunities to improve their lives. In addition, established housing and job patterns created black ghettos.

The SCLC decided to attack some of these problems in the city of Chicago, Illinois. Martin, along with other civil rights leaders, would have to go to Chicago. And this time, Coretta and the children would go with him and live in a slum apartment to dramatize the living conditions of most of Chicago's blacks.

The landlord had fixed the apartment up when he heard that Dr. King was planning to live there. Nevertheless, Coretta still described the place as grim. There was a strong smell of urine in the hallway, and the apartment itself was dingy and run-down. Outside, there was no park or even a clean place on the streets for the children to play. Under these conditions, Coretta watched the behavior of her children become worse. They fought more and often screamed at each other.

The Chicago program was not a total success. Many civil rights leaders believed that a city like Chicago was much too complex. The kind of nonviolent approach that Martin and the SCLC had used in the South simply did not work in such a large, diverse metropolis.

Martin felt sure he could change things in Chicago. He organized and worked with street gangs in the ghettos, held rallies, and planned a march to city hall. While these events were well attended, and some progress was made, ultimately Martin could not contain the anger and violence of some of Chicago's African Americans.

Besides violence, another problem Coretta faced in Chicago was apathy. The day after a riot, she spoke to a women's group at the Chicago YWCA. Coretta proposed that 100 women sign and send a telegram to Chicago's Mayor Richard Daley supporting Martin's proposals. No one seemed ready to sign. "What are you afraid of?" Coretta demanded of her audience.

Ultimately, the telegram was sent. A new, integrated organization came out of that meeting. It was called Women Mobilized for Change.

There were some major concessions made to blacks in the Chicago Freedom Movement. The mayor promised to clean up the slums and develop a policy for open housing and better job opportunities, but the agreement was never carried out.

After a summer of riots, broken glass, bullets, and shouts of "black power," it was a relief for the Kings to return to the calm of Atlanta and their home on Sunset Avenue. However, Coretta believed it had been an important experience for the children. It had exposed them, for the first time, to the horrors of northern ghetto poverty.

9

"You Must Be Prepared to Continue"

By 1967 Yoki, Marty, and Dexter were attending school. Coretta was becoming more confident and mature. Even though she was not as involved in her husband's work as she would have liked, she found ways to speak out and influence the movement. One of these ways was in her opposition to the Vietnam War.

Vietnam, a small nation in southeast Asia, had been fighting a civil war for many years before the United States became involved in the 1960s. At first, only a few U.S. advisors were sent to help the Vietnamese government fight against the communist rebels. China and Russia sent aid to the communist faction, centered in North Vietnam. The United States sent more equipment and then men to support the government side in South Vietnam. Before long, thousands of American soldiers, many of them African Americans, were fighting and dying in Vietnam.

Many young Americans did not want to fight in this war and protested United States involvement. Coretta was against all wars. Martin's philosophy of nonviolence coincided with her ideas. In

1965 Coretta was one of the speakers at a large peace demonstration in Washington, D.C. She urged the government to end its involvement in Vietnam.

Martin's antiwar statements were more of a problem. Some of his supporters believed that all Martin's efforts should go to helping their own people. Martin worried about dividing the civil rights movement, and so he kept his views to himself at first.

Coretta thought that Martin, as a Nobel Peace Prize winner, had a responsibility to take the lead in achieving world peace. Finally, goaded by his own conscience as well as by Coretta, Martin agreed.

On April 4, 1967, Dr. Martin Luther King, Jr., was among the speakers at Riverside Church in New York. The title of his speech was "Beyond Vietnam," and he openly and clearly opposed the war. Martin criticized the United States for its violence. He also pointed out that black people were dying in "disproportionate numbers" in Vietnam, reflecting their lower position in America.

Martin's stand against the war evoked much more criticism than Coretta's speeches. Prominent African-American leaders believed that Martin had hurt the civil rights movement by taking this stand. Martin's opinions, however, were not only based on what he considered best for the cause but also on his own moral commitment. He would not back down.

Eleven days after his speech, Martin participated in the Spring Mobilization for Peace in New York City. Coretta wanted to be there with him, but she had to speak at a rally for peace in San Francisco.

Coretta admitted to being disappointed. Again she would not be able to share an experience with her husband. She flew west to San Francisco and spoke before an audience of 50,000. But she would have preferred walking with Martin and the quarter million people who rallied in New York City.

Years later, biographers discussed Dr. King's doubts about the peace movement. They believed that he felt uncomfortable with the many extremists who burned the flag, destroyed their draft cards, and denounced the United States.

Coretta thought that Martin's participation in the drive to end the Vietnam War was a turning point for the peace movement and for the nation. Despite the criticism, Coretta viewed his call for peace as one of Dr. King's major contributions.

Martin and Coretta still felt strongly about helping the poor of all races improve their lives. In order to make the leadership in Washington more aware of the problems of America's poor, Martin and the SCLC leadership began to plan a campaign to directly involve poor people.

The Poor People's Campaign was another example of an idea that was thought of by many different people at the same time. Poor people would come to Washington, D.C., from all over the nation. They would set up tents right near the government buildings and confront the president and Congress with the reality of their problems.

Poor people, whether black or white, Hispanic or Native American, needed jobs and economic opportunities. Martin and Coretta were certain that lack of opportunity, poverty, and despair were the reasons for the riots that were occurring in the black ghettos of major U.S. cities. In order to raise money for this new campaign Martin once again traveled across the country making speeches and appealing for contributions.

It was not easy to raise money for this project. The problems of the civil rights movement were increasing. There were growing divisions and criticism among his own supporters, pressure from the FBI, and continued threats on his life.

Martin and his family lived under increased tensions. "If anything happens to me, you must be prepared to continue," Martin told his wife and co-workers. Although Coretta insisted in her autobiography that thoughts of death did not depress Martin, most of his biographers have disagreed. His closest colleagues reported that Martin was becoming more nervous and depressed. The pressure took its toll on his relationships with friends and family, and especially with Coretta.

With Martin traveling around the country, preparing for the Poor People's Campaign, Coretta and Martin had barely any time together. The following year was even worse. One writer described him as "plunging into the planning and organization of the Poor People's Campaign like a man possessed."

Even Coretta, always trying to protect Martin's image, acknowledged that her husband was under "intense strain" in the early months of 1968. She minimized her own surgery in January and her recuperation. Then they took a short vacation in Jamaica.

Historians believe that Martin was losing faith that the Poor People's Campaign would work. Since Martin's strong antiwar stand, many people had spoken out against him. It was harder than ever to raise the $400,000 needed for success.

Ralph Abernathy described Martin as "sad and depressed." Hosea Williams reported that Martin complained, "It just isn't working. People aren't responding."

In early February, Martin's anxieties were reflected in a famous sermon delivered at Ebenezer Baptist Church. "If any of you are around when I have to meet my day," Dr. King told his audience, "I don't want a long funeral." He went on to explain how he wanted to be remembered—not for the Nobel Peace Prize or any other prize he had received, not for his worldly recognition. "I'd like somebody to mention that day that Martin Luther King, Jr., tried to give his life serving others . . . "

Despite constant anxiety, Martin worked to recruit local leadership and convince poor people to join him in Washington. On one of those trips, Martin took his two sons with him. Later, Coretta thought that "Divine Providence" had intervened to give Marty and Dexter this special experience with their father.

Shortly after this trip Martin was invited to Memphis, Tennessee.

The Memphis protest began as an ordinary labor dispute by the mainly black Sanitation Workers Union. The repression of the strike by municipal authorities appeared to be directed against African Americans, and the Memphis branch of the SCLC supported the union cause.

Martin's first speech in Memphis was well received. It was like the old days of Montgomery and Birmingham, when he was able to unify all the black citizens. He promised to return and lead a protest demonstration on March 28, 1968.

That March 28 Coretta was in the nation's capital attending a press conference. The Women's International League for Peace and Freedom was urging the United States to make peace in Vietnam. On her way home she called SCLC headquarters in Washington, D.C., and heard that the Memphis march had become violent. Many protesters had been beaten by police, and one young man had been killed.

This was the first time that riots had broken out in a march that Martin led, and Coretta knew how disturbed he would be. She wanted to be home for him when he returned. Coretta remembered that they greeted each other with a kiss and had a quiet dinner together.

That night, Coretta described Martin as "sorrowful and disturbed." She tried to assure him that he was not to blame for the violence.

In spite of advice not to become further involved in the Memphis dispute, Martin could not withdraw. Here in Memphis, black workers—the worst paid city employees—were appealing for help. They needed his support. The next week, he and Ralph left once again for Memphis.

Many people who knew the Kings agreed that there were difficulties between Coretta and Martin at this time. They stemmed from the couple's different ideas about what Coretta's role should be. Martin believed strongly that his wife's place was at home, waiting for him. While Coretta tried to follow Martin's wishes, she was also eager to participate in the struggle. She pressured her husband to allow her to be more active.

An aide claimed that marital tensions between Coretta and Martin were a major cause of his depression. "That poor man was so harassed at home," he said, "that you cannot write about Dr. King without dealing with the reality."

Because Coretta was ready and eager to be there with Martin, it was difficult for her not to resent the time they spent apart. Waiting for her husband at home was not easy, either. She attended to innumerable details for Martin in his absence. The telephone rang until late at night. Guests came at all hours. Coretta could rarely relax and worried constantly. "In many ways she was a much put-upon person," conceded an associate.

Coretta has a different view of those few days with Martin. She saw him off to Washington, D.C., to attend to details of the Poor People's Campaign. When he returned they listened together to a broadcast of President Johnson's speech. The president announced his decision not to run for another term and urged the nation to negotiate for peace with communist North Vietnam.

The next day Ralph Abernathy came to pick Martin up for their return trip to Memphis. "I followed Martin to the door, kissed him goodbye and wished him well," wrote Coretta.

Despite a bomb threat on the plane to Memphis, Martin gave a moving speech that evening. It would become one of his most famous speeches, quoted in newspapers throughout the country. He ended it by saying, "We've got some difficult days ahead, but it really doesn't matter with me now. Because I've been to the mountaintop . . . and I've seen the Promised Land."

Martin remained in Memphis and waited for the march, scheduled for the following Monday. Doc—a nickname used for Martin by his fellow workers—stayed with his staff at the Lorraine Motel.

Thursday night, April 4, 1968, Martin was in good spirits. He came out onto the motel balcony, ready to go out to dinner. As he stood joking with his friends, a shot was fired from down below. Martin Luther King, Jr., was hit in the neck by an assassin's bullet.

Just as Coretta came home from shopping with Yoki, the phone rang. She heard the voice of Jesse Jackson, then a young worker in the civil rights movement. "Doc just got shot," he told her, but he was still alive.

It seemed to Coretta as if she had been waiting for this call for years. Still, she was in shock. Talking with Martin's aides on the phone, arranging to fly to Memphis, it all seemed unreal. With a police escort to the airport, provided by Atlanta's Mayor Allen, and friends and family accompanying her, she hurried down the airport corridor to the waiting plane. On the way, she heard her name over the loudspeaker and stopped walking.

Within moments, Dora McDonald, Martin's secretary and good friend, came toward her. She urged Coretta to come and sit down. At that instant Coretta knew. Her husband was dead.

She felt stunned and cold as she got back into the car, returning now to be with her children. With Martin's sister Christine Farris, her husband Isaac, and Mayor Allen, Coretta rode home in silence.

10

"I Am Acting in the Name of Martin Luther King, Jr."

"Should I hate the man who killed my daddy?" asked twelve-year-old Yoki, the tears streaming down her face. Martin would not want her to do that, Coretta answered. Then she had to explain as best she could to Marty and Dexter that their father was shot. The rest would keep until tomorrow.

Martin's death threw Coretta into a blur of arrangements. The funeral, memorial service, and burial would have to be carefully planned. Friends and concerned citizens tried to offer help and comfort. Reporters assigned to cover the event waited outside her house.

President Johnson phoned and told Coretta that he would convene Congress. He was planning to ask for a joint program of action on civil rights. Senator Robert Kennedy (who would be shot and killed a few months later) offered to fly her to Memphis. Harry Belafonte, long a close friend and supporter, came the following day, just to be with her and the children.

Despite the outpouring of support, Coretta remembered those

hours as a "nightmare night." The next day she flew to Memphis with a few friends to bring back her husband's body. At the airport there were crowds of people waiting to pay respects to the slain civil rights leader. But for Coretta, the hardest part was hearing her youngest child, Bunny, ask, "Mommy, where's Daddy?"

On Saturday, Coretta appeared at Ebenezer Baptist Church to make her first public statement to her husband's followers. She told the congregation that her religious faith had given her strength to bear the burdens. Her husband, explained Coretta, had given his life "for the poor of the world"—the garbage workers in Memphis as well as the peasants of Vietnam.

Many people heard Coretta King's words and remembered Martin's strong stand against violence. Others, in their grief and anger at his death, turned to destruction. Riots broke out in black neighborhoods in sixty-three cities throughout the United States.

With her family and friends to support and help her, Coretta somehow got through those first hours and days. Then on Monday she flew back to Memphis. She would walk in Martin's place at this final demonstration in support of the Sanitation Workers Union.

Coretta marched at the head of the line with Ralph Abernathy, Yoki, Marty, and Dexter beside her. She saw the silent, respectful crowds lined up along the route.

On the platform at Memphis City Hall, Coretta spoke mostly about Martin, telling her audience that he was "a great man, a great father and a great husband." She ended her speech optimistic in the face of this tragedy. Coretta still believed in a society of "love, of justice, peace, and brotherhood . . . "

The next day was the funeral. The children were dressed and waiting, and Coretta took a few minutes alone in her bedroom. Five minutes before they were due to leave she had one last guest. It was Jacqueline Kennedy, the widow of President John F. Kennedy, who had been assassinated five years before. To many people it seemed sadly appropriate that the wives of these two great leaders should be together.

At Ebenezer Baptist Church Rev. Ralph Abernathy conducted the funeral service. The church was jammed, and thousands more crowded the streets. Over 50,000 people from all walks of life came to pay their final respects.

The funeral and the few weeks that followed turned Coretta into a celebrity. Because the service was televised, people all over America were able to see and admire what newspaper reporters called Coretta's "quiet dignity," the "majesty of her bearing," and "her ability to endure the unendurable." There were also comments about Coretta's "motherly solicitude" and "the faultless behavior" of the King children.

When all the speeches, the visits, and the emergency help had ended, Coretta remained a visible presence in the community and in the nation. With Martin dead, the public turned to Coretta, the widow of the slain civil rights leader. Just days before she had insisted on a share in the work of the cause. Now she was thrown into a world of speeches and honorary degrees.

One month after the funeral, the rescheduled Poor People's Campaign was held in Washington, D.C. Ralph Abernathy, the new leader of the SCLC, was now in charge of this event. Poor people gathered from all over the United States. The aim of this multiracial march, Abernathy told a reporter for the *Atlanta Constitution,* was "jobs and guaranteed annual income."

Fewer people participated in the protest than the SCLC had hoped. It rained that whole week of May 1968, soaking the demonstrators in their tents and shacks, and tempers flared.

By the final day of the tent-in, with several major speakers scheduled to address the crowd, the rain had stopped. Coretta, who had also led a special "mother's march" against recent changes in the federal welfare laws, stepped up to the podium. She was greeted with thunderous applause by the 50,000 people in attendance.

In her speech Coretta warned that violence was "a madness" that would destroy society if it was not stopped. This was the closest Coretta Scott King ever came to a public show of anger or resentment about her husband's fate.

Shortly after the Poor People's Campaign, Coretta narrated "Lincoln's Portrait," a musical work by Aaron Copeland, at a Memorial Day concert in honor of Martin. Her performance was such a success that when the work was scheduled by the Washington National Symphony she was invited to repeat it.

At that time Coretta had little choice but to be busy. She not only had committed herself to furthering Martin's goals and protecting his image, but she also needed to support her family.

Coretta was to receive many honors after Martin's death. Here she and other prominent blacks receive honorary degreees from Bethune-Cookman College, a Florida college founded by Mary McLeod Bethune.

Most people were not aware of the King family's financial problems. Martin had given his life and energies to the causes of civil rights, world peace, and the poor of the world. He had put nothing aside for his children's education or his family's support. There was a scant $5,000 in their bank account and a life insurance policy, bought by Harry Belafonte, which provided another $50,000. It was one of many generous acts that helped Coretta and her children over the years. Even that money, however, was not enough to raise and educate four children. Honorary degrees were appreciated but offered no financial remuneration. Coretta needed a regular source of income.

Following Martin's death, the most promising opportunity was an offer by Holt, Rinehart & Winston, a major New York publishing company. If Mrs. King would write the story of her life, they would pay her more than $500,000. Coretta agreed. The result was *My Life With Martin Luther King, Jr.,* which was completed in 1969. The book recounted her life but emphasized the times she shared with Martin.

Reviews of Mrs. King's book were reserved. One reviewer referred to the "deliberate pages" that "document the movement." They described Coretta's writing much as they described her appearance: "dignified control," "restraint," and "spare narrative." There was general agreement that the widow did not reveal herself or her husband in this book.

"Did she never want to scream . . . " asked one reviewer in discussing Coretta's seemingly calm acceptance of her husband's— and her own—fate. A *Time* magazine review commented that Coretta's "wifely loyalty" robbed Martin Luther King "of the humanity of having faults."

Many people have wondered whether, after Martin's death, his wife put all the problems and conflicts of their daily life behind her. Coretta is a reserved and private person and has not shared her feelings freely. One interviewer suggested the reason was fear of being misunderstood. But Coretta's insistence that she was "strengthened by her husband's faith in the redemption of suffering" gives a hint of what goes on behind her calm exterior.

Coretta is also a practical and strong-willed person. She attacked the new problems of her life with a single-mindedness that amazed many people. At home in Atlanta, she quickly turned the bedroom of their red brick bungalow on Sunset Avenue into an office. This way she could be near the children while she worked.

Harry Wachtel, one of Martin's lawyers and close associates, spent many hours with Coretta after Dr. King's death. He became her business and legal advisor for several years and represented the family when the case of Martin's white murderer, James Earl Ray, came to trial. Neither Coretta nor anyone in the family wanted Ray to receive the death penalty. Following Wachtel's advice, Coretta chose not to be at the trial. An agreement was made that James Earl Ray would plead guilty to murder and get a life sentence.

After Martin's death, contributions poured in. Coretta decided that this money would be used to build a center in memory of Dr. King's philosophy of nonviolence. The announcement was made on January 15, 1969—Martin's birthday. It was the day when he would have been forty years old. Coretta explained that she wanted this memorial center to get beyond the black experience to all people who are "broken and oppressed . . . those who desperately search for justice, liberation, and peace."

Coretta envisioned an important and dignified center with a museum, library, and memorial, "a living monument to the peaceful warrior." She carefully filed away plaques, awards, and papers documenting the history of the civil rights movement. They were saved for the time when the Martin Luther King, Jr. Center would become a reality. When interviewers noted how few of Martin's personal memorabilia were in the Kings' living room, Coretta explained, "I was determined not to turn this house into a museum. As a family, we could not linger in his shadow . . ."

The year after Martin's death passed in a whirlwind of activity. Speeches took her all over the world. In India she accepted the Nehru Award, granted posthumously to her husband. In Italy, she had an audience with the Pope.

Over 150,000 pieces of mail arrived at the King home. Most expressed sympathy and solidarity with Dr. King's goals. Coretta, with the help of a staff of volunteers, tried to answer each one.

Shortly after Martin's death, she was elected to serve on the board of the SCLC, a position that afforded a small salary. Coretta's appointment, however, was more honorary than real. She did not feel at home at the SCLC offices and was not often invited there by the new leaders. She made speeches for the organization but was not included in policy decisions.

Coretta's life became a whirlwind of speeches. Here, she is pictured with African-American author Maya Angelou.

Coretta soon realized that some of her activities had to be limited. "I am not a ceremonial symbol," she told a reporter. "I am an activist. I didn't just emerge after Martin died—I was always there and involved."

Coretta refused to be what she called "an ornament" for any faction or group. She did accept one very special request. It was an invitation to speak at St. Paul's Cathedral in London, England. A few years before, on his way to Oslo to receive the Nobel Peace Prize, Martin had preached there and Coretta had proudly listened. Now she would be the speaker—the first woman ever to address an audience from the pulpit of St. Paul's. Even the Queen of England had never been honored in this way.

On March 14, 1969 Mrs. King and her four children left for London. When they landed, Coretta was tired and tense. Harry Wachtel remembers discussing her program for the next few days. It was one of the few times he ever saw Coretta angry, perhaps because she thought she had been overscheduled. But the airport was filled with newspaper reporters, photographers, and TV cameramen. Tired as she was, Coretta had to smile, pose for pictures, and answer questions before she was finally able to drive to her hotel and relax.

The speech at St. Paul's that Sunday was a great success. Going beyond the immediate concerns of black and white America, Coretta emphasized: "The time is now to feed the hungry of the world—whether they be in India, Biafra, Birmingham, Alabama or Birmingham, England." The very next day, Coretta spoke at Westminster Abbey in London. Again she talked about continuing her husband's work "to make all people truly free."

After an exciting few days, the Kings returned home. Coretta was satisfied with the trip but continued to worry about the children—not only about their behavior but also about their safety. The Kings had been subject to constant threats and were the victims of random violence too many times. First there had been the bombing of their home when Yolanda was a baby, the time Martin was stabbed in Harlem, and then his murder less than a year before. There was good reason for Coretta to worry about her children and to keep them, as Harry Wachtel said, "pretty much under her control."

Martin's father explained Coretta's attitude differently. "Coretta surrounded her children with love and guidance during a time when a lesser person's feelings might have torn her apart."

In 1970 John A. Williams wrote a biography about Martin Luther King and discussed the old stories about Martin's relationships with women. In response, Coretta told a reporter for *Ebony* magazine, "It's just one more attempt to kill Martin all over again."

Nevertheless, Mrs. King insisted she was not angry at Williams for reviving the rumors once more. "You see, they just can't hurt me anymore," Coretta explained, " . . . when your marriage is completely fulfilled, as ours was, you don't have to waste time worrying and harboring suspicions." Although few reporters or friends were convinced, people finally stopped asking Coretta about the rumors.

Coretta closed off this unhappy aspect of her husband's life, but she never forgot about Martin and the important ideas for which he stood. Her husband's dream, his goals for the country, his philosophy became more than ever a part of Coretta's being. "I am acting in the name of Dr. Martin Luther King, Jr.," she said over and over. His ideals motivated her and justified all her decisions.

Beginning in 1969, Coretta began to buy property on Auburn Avenue for the newly founded Martin Luther King, Jr. Center for Nonviolent Social Change. She had the help of an enthusiastic board of directors and a small amount of contributed funds. The first part of the center, the library reading room, was opened in October 1969.

Before dawn on January 14, 1970, just one day before Martin Luther King's birthday, Martin's body was moved. Coretta had been at this grave when Martin was first buried and several times since then. Today she was bringing him "home" to a place of honor. Soon a building and a permanent tomb would rise up around Martin's remains.

An article in *Jet* magazine stated that Coretta was "in love with her role as the person who is chiefly responsible for executing her husband's legacy." The editor wrote, "She possesses the self-sacrificing quality the project demands to carry out the Center's concept which seeks to serve all people."

But in addition to her dedication and self-sacrifice, Coretta Scott King had one more important quality. As she explained to another interviewer, "All my life I've thought there had to be solutions to problems, and I expected to be able to find them."

Coretta was often called on to make speeches. In 1971, she spoke at her alma mater, the New England Conservatory. Surrounding Coretta are her four children.

11

"The Right Time and the Right Thing To Do"

Five years after her husband's death, Coretta saw a different person when she looked in the mirror. Her face was fuller and more mature. An Atlanta newspaper wrote of her, "She usually looks sad, smiles infrequently and almost never laughs." But at forty-six, Coretta claimed she was more energetic than ever.

Alice Walker, a black poet and writer who visited with Mrs. King, observed that Coretta's eyes had changed. They were "reserved, almost cool," she said. She described Coretta as tense and guarded. Walker thought it was the "overwhelming publicity" that made it necessary for Coretta to keep her real feelings private.

Coretta carried herself with quiet dignity that encouraged formality. She was "Mrs. King" to her associates. "Corrie" was reserved for her family and friends. But underneath, her ideals were the same as those she had held twenty-five years before.

She would have done even more with Martin, Andrew Young acknowledged, but Martin "didn't want her to get too active." Young, Coretta's closest associate and advisor in the 1970s, acknowledged what many people always knew. "It was with great difficulty that he kept her in the home," he said of the late Dr. King. "He insisted both of them couldn't be gone all the time."

Coretta King often stated "I was an activist before Martin." She considered herself not only his wife but his co-worker. She saw the creation of the center as a living memorial to Martin as well as a continuation of her life-long goals. "My dream is the full development of the center," Coretta insisted.

Dreams alone were not enough to build the memorial center Coretta envisioned. Twenty million dollars was needed. Coretta and her staff had hoped to get help from the federal government in acquiring the land necessary for the project. However, the support pledged by President Richard Nixon never materialized.

Coretta was determined to obtain the money and make this dream a reality. She hired professional fund-raisers. She herself raised money by speaking throughout the United States and abroad.

By 1973 the general concept for the Martin Luther King, Jr. Center for Nonviolent Social Change had been submitted and approved, and a huge benefit concert was held in the Municipal Auditorium in Atlanta. A "Martin Luther King, Jr. Nonviolent Peace Prize" would be awarded to a different person each year to help draw attention to the center and its work. To design the actual building, a firm of architects was chosen.

Coretta and her family and friends remembered Martin each year on his birthday with a service at Ebenezer Baptist Church and Coretta's annual "State of the Dream" speech. But that was not sufficient. Coretta was determined to have the government establish a holiday in Martin's honor. In this way the rest of the nation would also remember.

Neither neglect from Martin's colleagues nor direct criticism stopped Coretta. Five years after her husband's death, she had become more forceful and sure of herself, forging ahead with plans.

She may have felt partly justified in her new role by the growing acceptance of the women's rights movement.

Feminism, or women's liberation, had followed on the heels of the civil rights movement. "The time is right for women to assert themselves in leadership positions," Coretta told a reporter, "to view themselves as a new and powerful creative force for social change. Women must begin to believe in themselves." Coretta was convinced that she should continue her husband's work. If she had doubts, she shared them with few.

The children remained Coretta's anchor, although she admitted to an interviewer that it was hard raising four children alone. She had carried most of the responsibility even while Martin was alive, but now she had added burdens.

"For a while," she recalled, "the children were afraid when I would go someplace." They worried that their mother, too, might get shot. Coretta remembered Marty telling her, "I understand about you having to do Daddy's work . . . but sometimes I wish I had two Mommies, one to write books and do Daddy's work and one to stay home with us."

Coretta felt sure that in spite of the hardships of their life, Yoki, Marty, Dexter, and Bunny understood. They wanted to continue their father's commitment to social justice. But first they each had to get the best education possible.

Yoki, the oldest, was graduating from high school and going North to Smith College, one of the finest women's colleges in the country. Marty would soon be going on to college, too. In spite of all that had happened, they were good children, not spoiled or self-centered.

When they were older, the children were often asked about how they were raised. "Mother had to be the disciplinarian, the one to instill values," Yolanda told an interviewer. Marty recalled, "My mother . . . taught us to be our own best self."

Work, studies, and commitment moved the King family along.

After Martin's assassination, her family rallied around Coretta. Daddy King, always strong, became even more important in the lives of his son's children. Coretta's sister Edythe came to be at Corrie's side after Martin was shot. Another staunch friend was Christine King Farris, Martin's sister.

Many positive changes were occurring in the state of Georgia in the 1970s. Jimmy Carter became governor and pledged to end discrimination in the state. Two years later, in 1972, he endorsed Andrew Young for congressman.

Jimmy Carter was already thinking of running for president by 1974. As a national candidate he reached out to the African-American community and tried to further the cause of racial equality. For the first time, the portraits of four of Georgia's prominent black citizens were displayed in the state capitol. At an impressive ceremony, Coretta unveiled the portrait of Martin Luther King, Jr.

By 1975 Daddy King, Andrew Young, and Coretta had all endorsed Carter as their choice for president. Carter won the Democratic nomination and went on to become president.

Andrew Young, who helped Carter win the black vote, was appointed United States ambassador to the United Nations. President Jimmy Carter also made the Martin Luther King, Jr. Center for Nonviolent Change one of his priorities.

Under Coretta's determined leadership, plans for the King Center continued throughout the 1970s, even when funds were less available. In 1975, with a large donation from the national chapter of Alpha Kappa Alpha sorority, the center renovated the home where Martin was born. Later that year, they arranged to have his birth home and Ebenezer Baptist Church entered on the National Register of Historic Places in the United States. Ground was also broken for the permanent entombment that would mark Martin's grave. The site included an interfaith chapel and what planners named a "Freedom Walkway."

In addition to buildings, there were also programs organized by the center to educate people in the ideals of nonviolence and civil rights. In 1974 the center launched a county-wide voter registration drive and organized a scholars internship program. This internship invited college students from more than twenty-five colleges in the United States and abroad for a semester of study at the King Center. They learned about the philosophy of nonviolence and worked with community organizations.

During those years, Coretta made unofficial visits to confer with leaders in Africa and India. In 1974 she was honored with a special medal, called the Ceres Medal. It was presented to her by the United Nation's Food and Agriculture Organization for her outstanding work on behalf of all underprivileged people.

That same year Coretta became one of the founders and the

Coretta recived the United Nation's Ceres Medal for her outstanding work on behalf of the underprivileged.

co-chairperson of the National Committee for Full Employment. This was "a high-ranking leadership coalition" with the aim of achieving full employment in America. "We must cease to be the only powerful, developed nation without a full employment policy," Coretta stated.

The National Committee for Full Employment consisted of labor unions and groups representing churches, minorities, and women. They organized meetings to educate the public about the problems of full employment, conducted research on how to achieve their goals, and lobbied Congress. As one of the leaders of this organization, Coretta attended meetings on Capitol Hill in Washington, D.C., and led giant rallies in New York City.

Coretta met with dignitaries everywhere, but the center was still her first commitment. A program of which Coretta was particularly proud was the first Summer Institute on Nonviolence in 1976, which became a yearly event.

So far, the modest accomplishments of the King Center had been achieved without large amounts of money or help from the United States government. Beginning in 1977, there was a major change. President Carter helped raise $3.5 million in federal funds for construction of the center. The efforts of the Ford Motor Company and its chairman, Henry Ford II, added another $4.7 million.

With this money, Coretta was able to fulfill her dream for the "living monument." She began what *Ebony* magazine described as "the Center's biggest project . . . the $8.5 million Freedom Hall complex." The complex would consist of two buildings that would include an auditorium, conference rooms, cultural center, and the King Library and Archives.

The four years of the Carter presidency were filled with activity and public appearances for Coretta. In 1977 she was appointed a member of the president's commission for the first National Women's Conference, to be held in Houston, Texas, in November.

President Carter also chose Coretta as one of three public

Coretta had always been an activist. Here she is seen at the first National Women's Conference, held in Houston in 1977.

delegates to the thirty-second General Assembly of the United Nations. The public delegates, selected for their past contributions to society, represented the United States at the U.N. General Assembly for one year. Coretta was able to renew her contacts with many of the African delegates. It gave her an opportunity to discuss King's ideas of nonviolence at the United Nations.

When the year at the United Nations was over, Coretta gave renewed attention to her primary goals. One of these was a determination to gain governmental support to make Martin's birthday into a national holiday. She was also committed to the growing Martin Luther King, Jr. Center for Nonviolent Social Change.

Coretta loved to talk about her work and her plans for the King Center. She explained that she wanted visitors "to feel that the

The Martin Luther King, Jr. Center for Nonviolent Social Change. Coretta's hard work helped make the center a reality.

During her time as a public delegate to the United Nations, Coretta participated in the annual Human Rights Day activities.

closest thing to Martin is his presence in this center. Actually, Martin doesn't need this, but the nation does."

Did Coretta need it? She had made the choice of "a life of service" early, and she never regretted it. However, in a rare, unguarded moment, Coretta confessed to a reporter that "there are times when I get tired and I wish I didn't have to do it." She admitted that sometimes she secretly longed to be able to go to concerts and plays, learn French and Spanish, and spend more time with friends. "I miss the stimulation," said Coretta, "I'm so absorbed in administrative detail."

Occasionally Coretta sat down to play the piano and sing, but those times were few. Her aspirations to be a concert performer were long forgotten. By 1980, with her children grown and gone from the house, Coretta made her work all-consuming.

President Carter had shared Coretta's goals for the King Center and wanted to help pass a bill to make Martin's birthday a national holiday. In spite of opposition, they had almost all the votes needed in Congress. Then Carter lost the 1980 election to Ronald Reagan.

President Reagan was disinterested. Nevertheless, Coretta Scott King did not give up. She traveled to Washington, D.C., gathering signatures on petitions and lobbying for the bill.

Representatives and senators were encouraged to vote for a Martin Luther King, Jr. Day. Senator Edward Kennedy, youngest brother of John and Robert Kennedy, was one of the bill's main supporters in the Democratic Party. Support from the Republican Party was also needed in order to make sure there would be enough votes. Finally, a few people from the Black Caucus, a political organization committed to helping elect African Americans to public office, approached Rep. Jack Kemp of New York and arranged a meeting with Coretta.

"She just poured out a sense of history," said Rep. Kemp. She spoke of " . . . what this meant to the country, how all Americans could benefit." Coretta convinced Kemp that "it was the right time and the right thing to do." He promised to get Republican votes, and he did.

By November 1983, sponsors of the bill proclaiming a national Martin Luther King, Jr. Day were sure of victory. Coretta was invited to sit in Congress and witness this historic event. It was the first time a black man would be so honored. The national, legal holiday was set for the third Monday in January. Celebration was scheduled to begin officially in 1986.

After the vote, there was the ceremonial signing by President Reagan in the Rose Garden. With Coretta's usual positive attitude, she declined to criticize the president publicly. Clouding this historic and exciting day, however, was Coretta's knowledge that until recently the president had resisted proposals for this holiday.

Coretta marched with Nobel prize winner Archbishop Desmond Tutu of South Africa and Mayor Andrew Young in the first annual Martin Luther King, Jr. holiday march.

12

"I Have Done Things . . .
Most Women Could Never Do"

Most black people are "much worse off" today than when Martin died, Coretta claimed. "Progress has been confined to a small number of people. We still have a long way to go."

Coretta spoke these words in Cincinnati, Ohio, in June 1983 as the keynote speaker at the annual YMCA Salute to Black Achievers. Coretta also announced a new march on Washington, commemorating the twentieth anniversary of the first march that Martin led in 1963.

That first march had culminated in his most famous "I have a dream" speech. Then, Coretta had stayed in the background. Twenty years later, she led the march, repeating the same route to the Lincoln Memorial. She saw her role as "carrying on the legacy." As the *Atlanta Constitution* had previously reported, "Keeping the dream alive is her vocation. Furthering the cause for which her husband died is her way of life."

Answering some critics who thought that the King Center was not helping the poor, Coretta firmly stated, "There has to be an institution that is teaching and promoting the idea of nonviolence. We are laying the foundation to train young leaders . . . in the tradition of Martin Luther King. When you have enough world leaders who have been exposed this way, it'll make a difference."

Despite Coretta's insistence that she is "committed to doing what is right and just for the advancement of humanity," complaints about her or the center have made her more reserved than ever. Coretta ignores the criticism. She just works harder and avoids confrontations. One of her basic strengths has been her persistent loyalty to Martin's ideas of nonviolent social change. She has "willed her life over" to her husband's philosophies, said a reporter in the *Atlanta Constitution* in 1986. Yolanda King clarified this statement, explaining "She not only married my father, she married his vision . . . she knows nothing else really."

The walls of her office are lined with awards from universities and civil rights organizations. There are photos of her with noted men and women who have sought her support. Famous entertainers have helped raised money for her cause. Coretta proudly admits, "I have done things that most women could never do."

In September 1986 Coretta travelled to South Africa to show her support for the black people's struggle for equality there. She met with many leaders, including Winnie Mandela, the wife of activist Nelson Mandela who had been in jail for twenty years.

Coretta came with the hope of acting as a peacemaker between the South African black people and the white government. Because of the complicated political situation, she did not succeed in bringing the two sides together. However, Coretta believed her visit was successful in other ways.

The meeting with Winnie Mandela was "one of the greatest and most meaningful of my life," said Coretta. Referring to Coretta, Winnie Mandela stated, "She is a symbol of what my people keep sacrificing for."

Many people in the United States knew, however, that Coretta was more than a symbol. Aware of how much she could accomplish, political leaders consistently asked for her support as a moderate African-American voice.

In 1988 Governor Michael Dukakis of Massachusetts and Rev. Jesse Jackson, a black man, were the principal Democratic candidates for president of the United States. Whoever won would run against Vice-President George Bush. Jackson had worked with Martin, but Coretta knew that he and her husband had many differences. She herself disagreed with Jesse in some ways, and Coretta remained neutral in this contest. She would not work for or support a leader only because he was black.

Coretta Scott King was invited to speak to the delegates at the Democratic Convention. Her tone was optimistic and hopeful as she discussed the progress black people had made in this country since the time of Martin's leadership. She turned to Jesse Jackson and said, "Martin would be proud of you, and we are all proud of you."

Coretta continued, "I come to this convention tonight . . . to remind you that for many Americans the dream is still deferred, despite the progress of the last twenty-five years." As Coretta's speech ended she urged: "I ask you, my friends, please do not forsake Martin's dream . . ."

Two months later Coretta and the SCLC president, Rev. Joseph Lowery, coordinated the twenty-fifth anniversary of the march on Washington. Marching on either side of Coretta were Jesse Jackson, Joseph Lowery, NAACP Director Benjamin L. Hooks, Jr., and presidential candidate Gov. Michael Dukakis.

The march focused on several issues, all important to Coretta. They were poverty, joblessness, world peace, and the downfall of the apartheid government in South Africa.

When Coretta spoke, she again recalled her husband's words and goals. "The festering sores of poverty, racism, war, and violence continue to frustrate our hopes for total freedom for all people," Mrs. King told the crowd at the Lincoln Memorial. "We are here today to say that we will not be turned around because we still have a dream . . . of a nation free from the cancer of racism and discrimination."

Coretta's children were also at this march. The older ones were each making some contribution to the center while pursuing their own lives. Bunny, the youngest, was still a student, attending Emory University in Atlanta. The King children attested to Coretta's devotion to family throughout her life.

Yolanda, together with Attallah Shabazz, daughter of Malcolm X, had established an acting group in New York City. The two women were also speaking in schools, dramatizing racial issues and trying to show solutions. Yolanda, now graduated from Smith

Coretta helped coordinate the twenty-fifth anniversary of the march on Washington. In this photo she stands with Jesse Jackson and Governor Michael Dukakis, among others.

College, spent part of her time in Atlanta as director of the Cultural Affairs Institute at the center.

Marty was involved in politics. He was a commissioner in Fulton County, Georgia and also director of the center's Youth Programs project.

Dexter, Coretta's second son, was director of the center's Office of Special Events and Entertainment when the 1988 March took place. Less than a year later there was a change. On Martin Luther King Day in 1989, Coretta King announced that she was resigning her post as president of the center. Dexter was going to take her place.

While Coretta would still be the chief executive officer and spokeswoman for the center, twenty-seven-year-old Dexter would manage the day-to-day operations. "I am extremely proud, and Martin would be proud of the decision that the board has made," announced Coretta at a press conference in Atlanta.

Dexter took over in April, on the anniversary of his father's death twenty years before. He promised that his goal was "to tackle the center's daily operations and mobilize the younger generation . . . The ideology will remain the same, but the methodology may change."

Andrew Young, Coretta's friend and supporter who was then mayor of Atlanta praised the move. He explained that it would allow Mrs. King "to travel and carry the center's message to national and international leaders and focus on securing the center's $40-million endowment."

The newspaper article that reported this change in leadership credited Mrs. King with "guiding the center from a basement operation into a complex with a $2-million budget, 63 staffers and national prominence." It was Coretta's efforts that had built the center. Now that it was a reality, it was hard for her to let it go.

Coretta conceded that she had difficulties in sharing authority with others. She admitted to being compulsive about attending to all the minute details by herself. "You can't hire folks to do your work for you," she once told an interviewer.

Four months after Dexter took office, a headline in the *Atlanta Constitution* announced "Dexter King Quits Amid Rift . . . Move is Linked to Infighting at Center."

There were many versions of the power struggle that ended in Dexter's resignation. "A little tension between generations," said Mayor Andrew Young. "Bureaucratic crossfire" and "factions and disorganization" said other sources.

Both Dexter and Coretta refused to make any statements to the press. There was no official reason offered to the public. Coretta remained silent until the following January.

In her report to the board of directors on January 13, 1990, Coretta avoided any display of feeling or regret about her son's actions. She referred to her past enthusiasm "about the future leadership of the King Center." Without ever mentioning Dexter's name, she explained, "At that time, we believed that the time was ripe for me to begin to turn over the mantle of leadership. . . . We now realize that it was not the fullness of time and that all things were not in place to move forward in this way."

On March 4, 1990, Coretta was involved with another anniversary march in Selma, Alabama. It marked twenty-five years since civil rights leaders had marched across the Edmund Pettus Bridge to aid in voter registration for blacks. That march had resulted in violence. Today, although there was still tension, conditions for African Americans had improved.

Marching over the bridge was Coretta Scott King, arms linked with many of Doc's aides from the old days. Rep. John Lewis, now a U.S. congressman from Georgia, Rev. Jesse Jackson, and Rev. Joseph Lowery, head of the SCLC, retraced the route of the first Selma protest of 1965.

The April 1990 issue of *Ebony* magazine listed the one hundred most influential black Americans. They included only people who headed major organizations and significantly affected the lives of large numbers of black people. Fifteen women were on the list, among them Coretta Scott King. She was referred to as "Chair and C.E.O. of the Martin Luther King, Jr. Center for Nonviolent Social Change."

In the opinion of many people in the black community, Coretta has moved into a new sphere of influence. She has risen beyond substituting for her husband and furthering his goals. Her own name is synonymous with civil rights and nonviolence.

Over the years Coretta has insisted on defining for herself the legacy that Martin Luther King left to the world. She has refused to allow anyone to alter her ideas of what Martin's dream was and what his memorial should be like. Because of Coretta, the King Center is imbued with a sense of black history.

Although sometimes criticized for not meeting the problems of the day, Coretta is steadfast in her vision for the center. The King Center teaches Dr. King's six principles of nonviolence. These are: accepting nonviolence as a way of life; trying to gain understanding through nonviolence; working to defeat injustice and not people; believing that "suffering can educate and transform people"; choosing love instead of hate; and believing that "the Universe is on the side of justice."

People who come to the center for training in King's six steps for nonviolent social change are first taught information gathering, which means knowing all sides of the issue, especially the opponent's position, and educating others to gain support and sympathy. Next comes making a personal commitment to work for justice by being ready to accept suffering if necessary. Finally, trainees must learn the art of negotiation in order to achieve the best results without humiliating the opponent and must understand direct action, which often means working with the opponent and reconciling all people involved.

Workshops that teach all these ideas are offered to institutional leaders, such as the representatives of American companies in South Africa, to police, and to young people.

In 1990, students were being trained in the six "Kingian" principles through a program administered by Coretta's youngest daughter, Bernice King. Bernice is a graduate of Emory University with a joint doctoral degree in divinity and law.

For several years, there has been a Kingfest. This is a series of outdoor, summer weekend entertainments organized by Yolanda King, which had attracted over 10,000 people.

When she is in Atlanta, Mrs. King tries to appear at each of the center's programs. But in the 1990s, Coretta's major goal is to obtain an endowment, a steady, guaranteed source of income for the center. To achieve this goal she travels a great deal, explaining her hopes for the center's future.

Coretta still maintains her ties to Africa. In the spring of 1990, she visited several African countries. Wherever she went, she was received with all the honors of a visiting dignitary.

In South Africa, Coretta again met with Winnie Mandela and her husband, Nelson, who had recently been freed from jail. She invited them to visit Atlanta during their trip to the United States. When Nelson Mandela came to the United States in June 1990, Coretta mobilized Atlanta for a full day in Mandela's honor and introduced him at various events.

This is Coretta at her best: organizing and successfully bringing people together. Perhaps she does not always get sufficient credit, but Coretta's aim is getting things done, not publicity.

In the years since Martin Luther King, Jr.'s death, Coretta has seen his methods applied on a grand scale. Nonviolent social change has been achieved in parts of the United States and most recently in Eastern Europe. As the government of Czechoslovakia was peacefully overturned, the Czech people sang "We Shall Overcome," the song made popular during the civil rights marches.

Coretta Scott King has kept Martin's dream alive and expanded his vision to embrace all people who strive for freedom. She has made a difference in the world and hopes to continue doing so. To Coretta, that means helping people and improving conditions in their lives. "I never thought I was going to save the world," she said, "but I felt that I could work and make some contribution to make things better for people who come after me."

Chronology

1927—Coretta Scott is born on April 27.

1940—Coretta begins attending the Lincoln School.

1942—The Scott family home burns down.

1945—Coretta is admitted to Antioch College.

1948—Coretta performs her first recital in Springfield, Ohio.

1951—Coretta leaves Antioch College to study at the New England Conservatory of Music.

1952—Coretta meets a young graduate student named Martin Luther King, Jr.

1953—Martin and Coretta are married in June.

1954—Coretta receives a bachelor of music degree in music education and voice from the New England Conservatory of Music.

She and Martin move to Montgomery, Alabama.

1955—Yolanda Denise is born on November 17.

The Montgomery bus boycott begins.

1956—The King house is bombed.

Coretta sings at several concerts to raise money.

The U.S. Supreme Court rules on November 13 that segregation in Montgomery's buses is unconstitutional.

1957—The Southern Christian Leadership Conference (SCLC) is organized on January 10.

Martin appears on the cover of *Time* magazine.

Coretta and Martin are invited to Ghana.

Prayer Pilgrimage for Freedom takes place in Washington, D.C.

Martin Luther King III is born on October 23.

1958—In September *Stride Toward Freedom* is published.

Martin is stabbed by a deranged woman.

1959—Coretta and Martin travel to India.

The King family moves to Atlanta, Georgia.

1960—Beginning of the sit-ins and the freedom rides.

Sen. John F. Kennedy arranges Martin's release from jail.

On November 8, Kennedy is elected president of the United States.

1961—Dexter Scott King is born on January 30.

1962—Martin becomes involved in the Albany protest movement.

Coretta attends the Disarmament Conference in Switzerland.

1963—Bernice Albertine King is born on March 28.

Martin is arrested during a protest in Birmingham; Coretta calls President Kennedy.

President Kennedy proposes a civil rights bill.

A new march on Washington is organized for August 28.

President Kennedy is shot and killed on November 22.

1964—Coretta's Freedom Concerts raise money for the SCLC.

Martin receives the Nobel Peace Prize.

The Civil Rights Act is passed and signed by President Johnson.

1965—Selma, Alabama, campaign begins.

Coretta joins Martin for the Selma to Montgomery march.

Voting Rights Bill becomes law on August 6.

1966—The King family spends the summer in a Chicago slum.

1967—Martin joins Coretta in her commitment to world peace; both speak out against the Vietnam War.

1968—The SCLC supports the labor dispute in Memphis.

Thursday evening, April 4, Martin is shot and killed.

Coretta speaks at the Poor People's Campaign in Washington.

1969—Coretta establishes the Martin Luther King, Jr. Center for Nonviolent Social Change.

She writes *My Life With Martin Luther King, Jr.*

1970—Martin's body is moved on January 14 to the new center.

Jimmy Carter becomes governor of Georgia.

1974—Coretta receives the Ceres Medal from the United Nations and co-chairs the National Committee for Full Employment.

1975—Coretta King endorses Jimmy Carter for president.

The center receives a donation and renovates Martin's birth home.

Ground is broken for Martin's permanent entombment.

1976—Jimmy Carter becomes president of the United States.

1977—Coretta begins building the center's Freedom Hall complex.

She is appointed as a delegate to the first National Women's Conference in Houston, Texas, then as one of three public delegates to the U.N. General Assembly.

1983—In November, the bill proclaiming Martin Luther King, Jr. Day is passed by Congress; Coretta speaks in Rose Garden.

1986—First national celebration of Martin Luther King, Jr. Day.

In September, Coretta travels to South Africa.

1988—Coretta speaks at the Democratic Convention.

She leads the twenty-fifth anniversary march on Washington, D.C.

1989—Coretta announces her resignation as president of the King Center; her son Dexter takes over.

On March 4, Coretta leads the anniversary march in Selma.

In April, Dexter resigns, and Coretta resumes her former position.

Coretta visits Africa again. She organizes Nelson Mandela's visit to Atlanta.

Further Reading

Abernathy, Ralph. *And the Walls Came Tumbling Down.* New York: Harper & Row, 1989.

Branch, Taylor. *Parting the Waters.* New York: Simon & Schuster, 1988.

Garrow, David J. *Bearing the Cross: Martin Luther King, Jr. and the Southern Christian Leadership Conference: 1955-1968.* New York: Morrow, 1986.

King, Coretta Scott. *My Life With Martin Luther King, Jr.* New York: Holt, Rinehart & Winston, 1969.

Morris, Aldon D. *The Origins of the Civil Rights Movement: Black Communities Organizing for Change.* London: Free Press, 1984.

Oates, Stephen B. *Let the Trumpet Sound: The Life of Martin Luther King, Jr.* New York: Harper & Row, 1982.

Patterson, Lillie. *Coretta Scott King.* Champion, Ill.: Garrard, 1977.

Robinson, Jo Ann Gibson. *The Montgomery Bus Boycott and the Women Who Started It.* Knoxville, Tenn.: University of Tennessee Press, 1987.

Schulke, Flip, ed. *Martin Luther King, Jr.: A Documentary—Montgomery to Memphis.* New York: Norton, 1976.

Vivian, Octavia. *Coretta.* Philadelphia: Fortress Press, 1970.

Williams, John A. *The King God Didn't Save.* New York: Coward, McCann, 1970.

Sources For Chapter Titles

Introduction—"The Blessing of His Life" *The New York Times,* Nov. 3, 1983, p. A28, quoting from Coretta's speech in the Rose Garden.

Chapter One—"As Good As Anyone Else." *My Life with Martin Luther King Jr.,* p. 34, quoting Coretta's mother Bernice Scott.

Chapter Two—"Wherever Martin Lives, I Will Live There Too." *My Life with Martin Luther King Jr.,* p. 70, quoting Coretta.

Chapter Three—"Much Bigger Than Montgomery." *My Life with Martin Luther King Jr.,* p. 123, quoting Coretta.

Chapter Four—"Our Faith Has Now Been Vindicated." *My Life with Martin Luther King Jr.,* p. 146, quoting Martin's sermon.

Chapter Five—"Lord, I Hope This Isn't the Way Martin Has To Go." *My Life with Martin Luther King Jr.,* p. 167, quoting Coretta.

Chapter Six—"Everything We Can to Help." *My Life with Martin Luther King Jr.,* p. 196, quoting Senator Kennedy.

Chapter Seven—"Watch it, Man, That's Mrs. King." *My Life with Martin Luther King Jr.,* p. 240, quoting one of King's guards at a march on Washington.

Chapter Eight—"I Have to Resist Worry." *My Life with Martin Luther King Jr.,* p. 261, quoting Coretta's remark to a friend.

Chapter Nine—"You Must Be Prepared to Continue" *My Life with Martin Luther King Jr.,* p. 304, quoting Martin.

Chapter Ten—"I Am Acting in the Name of Martin Luther King, Jr." Article from the King Center.

Chapter Eleven—"The Right Time and the Right Thing To Do." *Washington Post,* Jan. 19, 1986, p. K4, quoting Rep. Jack Kemp.

Chapter Twelve—"I Have Done Things . . . Most Women Could Never Do." *Detroit News,* 1983, Burrelle's "Profiles in Power" column.

Index

125

127

About the Authors

Sondra Henry is a graduate of Columbia Law School, and practiced law for many years. Emily Taitz is completing her Ph.D. in Jewish history at the Jewish Theological Seminary of America. Together they have taught courses on women's history and coauthored several books, including *Betty Friedan: Fighter for Women's Rights* for Enslow Publishers.